THE 7
DEADLY
MYTHS

**ANTISEMITISM FROM THE TIME
OF CHRIST TO KANYE WEST**

Cherry
Orchard
Books

ALEX RYVCHIN

THE 7 DEADLY MYTHS

**ANTISEMITISM FROM THE TIME
OF CHRIST TO KANYE WEST**

BOSTON
2023

Second edition, revised and supplemented

Library of Congress Control Number: 2023943764

ISBN 9798887193304 paperback
ISBN 9798887193311 ebook PDF
ISBN 9798887193328 epub

Book design by PHi Business Solutions
Cover design by Anna Mardakhaeva
Cover photo © Martine Payne Photography

Published by Cherry Orchard Books, an imprint of
    Academic Studies Press
1577 Beacon Street
Brookline, MA 02446, USA

press@academicstudiespress.com
www.academicstudiespress.com

For my mother and father

Contents

Acknowledgements

This book came about in a somewhat unusual way. I had written an article for *Newsweek* about the antisemitism issue that was afflicting the British Labour Party and pitting its then leader, Jeremy Corbyn, against the Jewish community. Life was becoming near on intolerable for many British Jews as a result. After the piece was published, I received an email from Dr Gus Lehrer, an eminent mathematician and a pillar of the Australian Jewish community, asking to meet to discuss my piece. Gus liked what I had written, and we discussed how antisemitism was resurgent even among the supposedly enlightened. It was the last form of racial hatred that one could openly profess in civilized society.

The culmination of my conversations with Gus and thinking on the issue was the idea for *The 7 Deadly Myths*—a concise and hopefully entertaining book that identifies the myths that cling tenaciously to Jews and consciously or unconsciously determine how they are perceived. Something that could be used as a resource for students, educators and policymakers and a collection of fascinating stories of baffling conspiracy theories, odious figures and the devastation they together inflicted, and continue to inflict.

Gus Lehrer deserves credit for setting me on the road to writing this book and for his encouragement and generosity. I wish to thank Dr John Kennedy too, and Jillian Segal and John Roth for so generously supporting the online resources that accompany this book.

There are many others who deserve credit for this book. The Executive Council of Australian Jewry, the organization I am privileged to serve as its co-Chief Executive Officer, is one of the world's most important and effective institutions in the struggle against antisemitism. It was a global leader in the fight to liberate Soviet Jewry, of which I am a personal beneficiary, it has doggedly pursued Holocaust deniers, and it unites the community in the struggle for Jewish rights. An organization is the sum of its history and its individuals. I want to therefore thank each of its past presidents, especially those I have had the immense good fortune to know and work with, the late Isi Leibler, Jeremy Jones, Nina Bassat, Danny Lamm, Anton Block and most of all the tireless and brilliant Robert Goot. I want to thank co-Chief Executive Officer Peter Wertheim, a kindred spirit who lives in the service of the community and the Jewish people. Foremost, I want to thank Jillian Segal. Jillian possesses the clearest qualities of leadership I have been able to observe in another person—vision, strength, tenacity, excellence, integrity, sound judgement and selflessness. As president of the Executive Council of Australian Jewry she has propelled the organization to new realms, including pioneering programs in education, implemented structures for succession such as the Jewish Advocacy & Leadership Corps and developed a modern advocacy and communications function that enables the Jewish people to tell their stories and to pierce the ignorance and malice that surrounds them. Jillian has also helped me immensely through her support for my writing and her trust in my abilities. The Jewish people owe much to Jillian Segal, as do I.

I want to thank my wife, Vicki, for walking beside me in life, bringing happiness and love to every day of my life and indulging me in my ramblings. She suffers daily when my mind escapes to odd places like Napoleon's Assembly of Jewish Notables and the offices of the Judenrat in Warsaw in search of things I will never find. I hope she at least enjoys the observations I bring back with me. I thank my three daughters Lilah, Elly and Maya who have taught me the meaning of life, to love and be loved. They bring purpose, pride and wonder to my life. They have made it immaculate. I thank my grandparents Lucy and Zakhar for their iron wills and their stories. I thank my brother, Eugene, of the highest and most blessed memory, the finest human being I have ever known, for teaching me to live with purpose, courage and fun. Finally, I want to thank my parents, Michael and Tanya, to whom this book is dedicated, for giving me a love of my people, a hatred of antisemitism, and for every conversation about Soviet history, every piece of advice I scoff at but eventually adopt, and every precious moment in their company.

Introduction
Understanding Antisemitism

———————

Antisemitism is not easily understood because the Jews themselves are not easily understood. They are bound by ethnicity,
even common genetic markers, yet a convert to the faith is a
fully fledged and accepted Jew. They hold to ancient texts and
religious traditions such as male circumcision and the laying
of Tefillin, yet a Jew entirely devoid of these practices remains
a Jew and can express their Jewishness in other ways. This in
itself is a source of animosity. We tend to fear that which we
cannot easily place.

This manifold nature of being Jewish, something that
evolved through millennia, shaped by extraordinary experiences and developed in a homeland, then a diaspora, and then
in both, means one can customize how they live as a Jew. It
also means antisemitism can be customized to adhere to one's
worldview. One can display an intense hatred of the Jewish
religion but exhibit no animosity towards Jews as an ethnic
group, as occurred in the case of early religious antisemitism.
One could intensely hate the Jews as an ethnic group but
care nothing for their religious preferences, as in the case of
Nazism. And one can adorn the State of Israel with all manner
of antisemitic conspiracy theory yet hold Judaism and Jewish
culture in high regard, as has become common in some sectors
of the far left.

For as long the Jews have been a people, they have been treated as a problem to be solved. Can this stubborn nation be absorbed into the great empires that came to rule over them? Can these original monotheists be allowed to live alongside Christianity and Islam? What is to be done with these wandering internationalists who for nearly two millennia possessed no country of their own? Can the Jew be a Frenchman? A German? An Arab? Can the Jew assimilate or are their eyes permanently cast east towards a lost homeland and downward at ancient texts? Does the Jew belong to a race, a religion or a nation?

The Jewish enigma has aroused some measure of benign curiosity, even some reverence. But overwhelmingly the Jews aroused fear and suspicion. In the pages that follow, we will find men for whom antisemitism became a creed, an evangelizing mission. These individuals could manipulate those fears and suspicions and recruit others to the cause of bringing the Jews low, seeing them humiliated and destroyed. Why did they want this? It is impossible to understand. We search for a Jew in the lineage as if killing the Jews is an act of self-mutilation or self-purification. Perhaps a Jewish former lover. A personal slight. All of these inquiries prove unsatisfactory as they seek rational answers to the fundamentally irrational.

There are many characteristics of antisemitism that cannot be found in other forms of hatred. But this power to consume the hater as much as the hated, to turn bigotry into a monomaniacal quest, is surely its most distinct quality.

Antisemitism has summoned populations to burn their neighbors at the stake. It has motivated monarchs to uproot and expel entire communities. And it compelled a dictator, for whom antisemitism was his all, to unleash the most devastating war in human history. It loaded the gun of Robert Bowers, who murdered eleven worshippers in a Pittsburgh synagogue in 2018. Antisemitism has caused civilizations to decay with irrationalism and has polluted minds with puerile conspiracy theories.

Antisemitism has also personally touched every Jew. In the early years of my life in Australia, I had little firsthand exposure to antisemitism. It accompanied me only as a vestige of my family's former life in the Soviet Union, something I could feel but not quite see. My family had left the Soviet Union as refugees when I was three years old. Our eventual freedom, and that of millions of families like mine, was the culmination of a decades-long international campaign under the banner "Let my people go," which pressured the Soviet Government to allow its Jewish population to leave.

As the Australian diplomat Douglas White put it when raising the matter at the United Nations, "should the USSR find difficulty in according Soviet Jewry full freedom to practice their religion, it has a moral obligation to permit them to leave the country."[1]

Of course, the Soviet Union would never freely admit it denied anything to anyone. The official Soviet position was that antisemitism belonged to the previous regime and any suggestion that the Jewish population faced institutional racism was just Cold War-era mischief making. In reality, Soviet

---

[1] "Persecution of Jews in Russia," Prime Minister's Department, A1209/111, item 62/963, 26 October 1962, National Archives of Australia (NAA), quoted in Sam Lipski and Suzanne Rutland, *Let My People Go: The Untold Story of Australia and the Soviet Jews 1959–1989* (Melbourne: Hybrid Publishers, 2015), 90.

Jews suffered immensely. Their identity papers were marked as "Jewish" regardless of how long families like mine traced their roots in those lands, or how integrated they strived to be. Aside from having no freedom to practice their faith, Jews were subjected to racial restrictions, including entry quotas into universities, thereby excluding them from certain professions, and a prohibition on Jewish cultural practices including the printing of Hebrew-language publications. No other nationality or ethnic group suffered such measures.

This institutional antisemitism began in Tsarist times and had established the Jews as people of no worth, to be ridiculed and discarded. In George Orwell's *Down and Out in Paris and London*, a retired Russian army officer tells Orwell how in the army it was considered poor form to spit on a Jew "because a Russian officer's spittle was too precious to be wasted on Jews."[2]

In the seventeenth century, the Ukrainian nationalist figure Bogdan Chmelnitski and his horsemen unleashed such carnage on Jewish communities that to read the accounts of them leads one to call humanity into question. These crimes set a certain rhythm whereby any upheaval, any discontent, any pursuit of political transformation resulted in Jewish communities being set upon with a perverted delight and with total impunity. It happened throughout the nineteenth and early twentieth centuries often at the instigation of the authorities. It happened during the civil war that followed the Bolshevik Revolution. And it happened during the Nazi invasion of the Soviet Union, resulting in some 1.5 million Jews disappearing

2   George Orwell, *Down and Out in Paris and London* (Melbourne: Text Publishing, 2016), 48.

in forest pits and ravines and burning warehouses, through every method of torturous and unnatural death imaginable.

The permanent fear of mob violence and the injustice of racist laws was a fact of life but the vulgarity and public humiliations the Jews experienced in the street, on the trolleybus, in the shop queue, stung bitterly and daily. It was not uncommon for irate citizens standing in futility to buy basic necessities to break out into curses and cries about the Jews. "If there's no water in the taps, the Jews drank it all," was one common refrain. "Beat the Jews, save our Russia," was another. Every Jewish boy had taken regular beatings in the schoolyard. My father's lunchtime football games would quickly descend into spirited bouts of "catch the Jew." My grandmother had once thrown herself upon her elder brother's prone body to protect him from the boots of antisemitic thugs that were striking his ribs and skull. My mother, who lived a block away from a Holocaust-era killing field in Kyiv known as Babyn Yar, experienced antisemitism like a daily ritual. As her trolleybus approached her destination and the conductor called out, "next stop, Babyn Yar," every day, without fail, one of the drunks dozing peacefully would suddenly return to lucidity, sit bolt upright, and cry out and cackle and lament, "if only they'd shot all you Jews here!"

Only once did my mother see this behavior go challenged. An army officer in uniform berated the drunk for celebrating the deaths of fellow citizens, for which the officer was turned upon by his fellow travellers, receiving their howls and insults for his unpatriotic conduct.

My father would tell me of how admired he was by his pupils in the town high school where he taught math and physics. He was a young, dynamic and passionate teacher. Then one day, a rumor circulated the schoolyard, that he, their beloved mentor, was in fact a Jew. The students filed into his office, one by one, to ask if this was really so, and to offer their condolences. "But how could this be?" one boy asked him with great earnestness, "you're such a good person."

As a boy, my father had made the mistake of asking one of the old town matriarchs why the area on the edge of the town limits was called a ravine when it was in fact completely flat. "Ah my boy," she answered with great pride, "it was a ravine, until we filled it with Jews." My father had once asked his father why he kept an axe permanently positioned by the front door. He had never seen it used. His father took a sharp breath, sat his son down and asked him if he knew the word "pogrom."

Eli Wiesel survived the hellscape of Auschwitz and became a Nobel Laureate for a body of written work so soulful, it somehow heightens the sorrow of the Holocaust to know one as sensitive and beautiful as Wiesel was subjected to it. In the 1960s he travelled to the Soviet Union, including to my birthplace of Kyiv, to see for himself the conditions under which the Jews there lived. He then recorded his observations in a book titled *The Jews of Silence.*

Wiesel wrote that one thing struck him about the Jews there above all others. It was their fear. Fear inhabited the eyes of every Jew he encountered without exception. That fear came from the individual traumas described, some variation of which had been experienced by every Jew. But it also came from a collective panic from opening the papers to see the "rootless cosmopolitans" and "Zionist bankers" denounced, cartoons of great hook-nosed creatures preying upon the decent citizens of the state, or to read of the Night of Murdered

Poets when Jewish artists and actors were rounded up, tortured and murdered under Stalin's orders. The fear was deep and generational.

Leaving the Soviet Union at the age of three, I of course had no personal experience of any of this. I carried no obvious trauma, nor did I, to my knowledge, exhibit the fear that Wiesel had observed. But I witnessed this in my parents and grandparents. It was not just in the stories they told me; those stories that were shaping my own consciousness and sense of self, but through their inherent, involuntary actions. The fear and trauma are not easily dislodged, not even by the safety and distance of Australia. It presents as a sort of nervous energy, a perpetual sense of looming calamity, a tendency to experience joy as an interval between disasters, and a stiffening of the face the second the word "Jew" is heard.

Aside from some fairly harmless schoolyard run-ins, my childhood was free of antisemitism. When it did occur, it was momentarily jarring but mostly left me perplexed, seeking to decipher what was said and what or who had prompted it. At tennis practice a boy of no more than ten once came up to me and said, "Jewish, ewww." In primary school, a classmate, who had clearly been well briefed, gave me a good dressing down for "being strange" for being a Jew. I can recall he was highly animated, flailing even, face fixed in a hawkish sternness rarely seen in the prepubescent. Strange indeed.

In high school, I regularly heard "Jew" used as a verb, as in "so and so got Jewed," or "he's trying to Jew you." These incidents didn't scar me or cause undue distress. They were unpleasant, but I had by that point come to understand what real antisemitism was, and it was not that.

My family moved house every couple of years as new migrants finding their way tend to do, and in my early teenage years we came to live in a modest apartment block in middle class Randwick in Sydney's eastern suburbs. Directly above us lived a couple who had migrated from Austria. The man was ageing but tall and vigorous, with a deep resonant voice and a farmer's build. When he met my father, who spoke with a strong Russian accent and whose pale blue eyes and fair complexion hardly betray his ethnicity, the neighbor was genial to a fault. He even offered to lend my father any tools he might need to get settled in. Then he saw my mother, and everything changed.

The neighbor's name was Kurt Rosenberger and upon learning that the new occupants were Jews, he would stand on his balcony and bellow at us, night after night, alternating between a thunderous guttural roar and a sneering tone full of menace, "Hitler didn't finish the job, I will finish it for him." An evening serenade that continued for weeks. It was plainly terrifying to hear. It became difficult to sleep beneath such a man, and it pained me to see the fear that returned full bore to my parents' eyes.

Why did he hate us so? What did he think we had done? What did he think we intended to do beyond living simple, honest lives as hopeful migrants in a new land?

He surely would have had no coherent answer to these questions. He probably didn't ponder on them a great deal. But he knew with perfect certainty that the Jew, represented in that moment by my parents and their two boys, was something so loathsome, so repugnant, so unhuman, that he was justified in behaving in such a manner to an ordinary young family.

In every other stratum of his life, Kurt Rosenberger would have been a perfect gentleman, a man of deep morality, wholesome values, an even disposition. Owners board, neighborhood watch, that sort of thing. I often saw him engaging in civil banter with the couple across the road. How was it that when placed in the mere vicinity of a Jew, he was moved to such fury, such frenzy as to threaten repeatedly to kill a family?

In many ways, this is the same question that philosophers, historians and social scientists have posed when attempting to make sense of the Holocaust. How did a country as advanced and enlightened as twentieth-century Germany make anti-semitism its national idea, deploying its magnificent energy and full force to pursue every Jew, even those thousands of miles away, until they were nearly obliterated from the face of the earth? How did many thousands of ordinary people all across Europe choose to join killing squads, volunteer to form search parties to comb the forests, and dispossess, humiliate and murder their neighbors simply because they were Jewish? How did elite soldiers, educated, Church-going men in their thirties, perform actions such as throwing Jewish children into pits of quicksand and hurling sweets at them gaily as they flailed and suffocated before their eyes?

We imagine them carrying out their missions with a robotic efficiency. But accounts of the method of the killings, testimonies of perpetrators, witnesses and survivors, tell a story of revelry, of jolly good sport. One of the few Jews who crawled out of the river of blood that was the Babyn Yar killing site, recalled the soldiers "laughing as if they were watching a circus act." Thousands of Ukrainians, Belarusians and Balts volunteered to join killing squads or for special assignment at the death camps. "Trawniki men," they were called. They tended to parade around the camps, mocking the Jews standing in line for the gas chambers, hacking off breasts with their swords, driving rifle butts through unassuming skulls, purely for the thrill of it. In Kaunas, the Jews were paraded in a carpark as a young Lithuanian man bludgeoned Jews to death with a crowbar in front of a crowd that sung the national anthem and cheered every killing. The standard defense of following orders just doesn't seem to do.

There were reports of German SS men asking to be transferred out of their units due to the psychological toll of hunting and killing innocent people, day after day. There is not a single record of such a request being met with demotion or disciplinary action. Yet few made such requests. No doubt they found the work interesting. Marauding through the verdant Soviet countryside in cars and on motorbikes, like merry adventurers, clad in leather, those immaculate German uniforms, carrying out "special measures," under direct orders of the Chief of the Security Police, Reinhard Heydrich. They were sleuths and game hunters all at once. They carried out their work with an almost majestic efficiency, sending back daily reports of their accomplishments: 875 Jewish girls and women shot in Berdychiv; ninety Jewish children shot in Bila Tserkva; 33,771 in Kyiv; 23,600 in Kamianets-Podilskyi.

Paul Blobel, who commanded the killing squad in Kyiv, was driving a fellow SS man to dinner one evening when his companion noticed some peculiar disturbance in the soil of a field they were passing. "Clumps of earth rose into the air as if by their own propulsion—and there was smoke; it was like a low-toned volcano; as if there was burning lava just beneath the earth. Blobel laughed, made a gesture with his arm pointing back along the road and ahead, all along the ravine—the ravine of Babyn Yar—and said, 'Here lie my thirty-thousand Jews.'"[3]

The answer to why many thousands of fairly unremarkable people, of different nations, professions, languages, religious sects, social classes, each devotedly carried out these acts lies in the cumulative effect of two millennia of conspiracy theories that explicitly bound the Jews up with every evil in our world—money, war, disease, trickery, arrogance, bloodthirstiness, even the killing of God. This was presented, virtually from birth in the form of vivid storytelling, searing sermons, classical literature, glorious art and carefully calibrated propaganda that appealed to human fear and psychological frailty.

This transformed the Jew from an individual human being, bound, often extremely loosely, to other Jews by ancestral, cultural, religious associations, possessing all the flaws and virtues with which each person is endowed, into something that is at once vastly inferior and terrifyingly dangerous. In other words, vermin. And as the Holocaust historian Yehuda Bauer said, "one does not argue with vermin."[4]

The crimes of our time occur through this same well-honed process. One October morning in 2018, a man named Robert Bowers, a frequent poster of standard white supremacist fare on social media, entered the Tree of Life Synagogue in Squirrel Hill, Pittsburgh during the Sabbath service, armed with a semi-automatic rifle. Bowers took his aim and shot eleven Jews dead.

---

3   Gitta Sereny, *Into That Darkness: From Mercy Killing to Mass Murder* (London: Pimlico, 1974), 97.

4   Yehuda Bauer, *The Holocaust in Historical Perspectives*, (Canberra: ANU Press, 1970), 9.

Who were the people he shot? Rose Mallinger, ninety-seven years old. Jerry Rabinowitz, a doctor who treated AIDS patients during the height of the epidemic. One patient recalled, "he often held our hands (without rubber gloves) and always, always hugged us as we left his office." Cecil and David Rosenthal, brothers with intellectual disabilities, they were inseparable and never missed a service. David Stein, seventy-one, who had just become a grandfather. Richard Gottfried, a dentist who had sought solace in his faith following the death of his father. Joyce Fienberg, a retired research specialist. Melvin Wax, eighty-eight, a retired accountant who loved the Pittsburgh Pirates. Sylvan and Bernice Simon, killed in the same synagogue they were married in more than sixty years before. Irvin Younger, a grandfather who volunteered at the synagogue. Bowers didn't see doting grandparents, loving brothers or the Pittsburgh Pirates. He saw only vermin. He was doing the world a favor.

In the eyes of my old neighbor, Kurt Rosenberger, I wasn't a kid concerned with the petty debauchery and idleness that fills the teenage mind. I was a roach that had crawled into his line of sight and had to be exterminated, because unfortunately, as Kurt had lamented to us, Hitler had left some loose ends. Maybe Kurt himself felt he had some unfinished business: he would have been of fighting age after all.

Very many books and articles have speculated as to the question of "why?" Why have the Jews been so despised and so brutalized throughout history? "Why" is a necessary and logical question and this book, I believe, will go some way to answering it. At the very least, it will offer an understanding of historic and present antisemitism, its evolution, proponents, methods, consequences and so on, from which the reader can contemplate their own "why?"

Hannah Arendt believed that the Jew is a convenient scapegoat who has suffered from totalitarianism, but it could just as easily have happened to any other ethnic group. Maybe it could have, but it didn't.

Jean-Paul Sartre theorized that the antisemite does not hate the Jew for who he or she really is, but instead hates the mythical Jew he himself conjures to lay all ills of modernity and a rapidly changing world upon some living, breathing creature. There is something to this, though Sartre goes on to dismiss a distinct Jewish national consciousness, arguing that Jews are bound by their suffering and nothing more. With this, I profoundly disagree.

Then there is perhaps the most common explanation that antisemitism comes from jealousy for Jewish success. Jews are perceived to be uniformly wealthy and successful—itself a problematic formulation—and Jews have made considerable contributions to innumerable disciplines and fields.

Beyond the writers, the Nobel laureates and the scientists is an altogether more impressive achievement: their survival. They have survived from antiquity to modernity virtually unchanged in their national and religious customs. They have outlived the empires and war machines that sought to annihilate them. They regained their independence despite two millennia of dispersal and exile. Kurdish, Tibetan and Assyrian leaders, fellow ancient peoples who lost their homelands, have spoken of the Jewish experience as the exemplar for how to remain a people despite seeing ancestral lands pass into the hands of others, and how to form a successful movement of national return.

The Dalai Lama said, "we always talk of the Jewish people scattered in so many countries, speaking so many languages. Yet the Jews keep their traditions. It is something very admirable."[5]." The Korean Ambassador to Israel declared to an incredulous Israeli audience, "each Korean family has at least one copy of the Talmud. Korean mothers want to know how so many Jewish people became geniuses. Twenty-three percent of Nobel Prize winners are Jewish people. Korean women want to know the secret. They found the secret in this book."[6] A Chinese scholar observed that "the Jewish people have developed a tough, confident and incisive character and a culture that highlights creative thinking, practicality and pursuit of knowledge and truth."[7] These views provide some hope, but they are far from the norm; outliers that tend to bemuse more than anything.

Is this success, real or perceived, the cause of antisemitism? No. Success does not automatically arouse hatred. We admire those we consider worthy of success. We only despise those we consider undeserving.

Then there is the new dogma coming out of sociology departments along the lines that antisemitism is just one form of racism, all racisms are by-products of colonialism and power imbalances and cannot be defeated unless they are all defeated together—a proposition that completely dismisses

---

5   Ari L. Goldman, "Dalai Lama Meets Jews from 4 Major Branches," *New York Times*, September 26, 1989.

6   Ross Arbes, "How the Talmud Became a Best-Seller in South Korea," *New Yorker*, June 23, 2015.

7   Song Jian, "Chinese Jews and China-Israel Relation," *Chinese Studies* 3 (2014): 121–127.

the uniqueness of antisemitism, and essentially applies the "all lives matter" treatment to the ongoing torment of the Jews.

A more mystical explanation is to be found in the Talmud which traces antisemitism to Mount Sinai, where the Jews received the laws that formed the basis of western ethics. The Hebrew word for hatred is nearly identical to Sinai, "sinah." Perhaps the sinah that came from Sinai is a form of jealousy, perhaps it is the spirit of rebellion against purported teachers and lawgivers.

The hatred of the Jews is patently unique. There is the longevity of it. The ubiquity of it. The fanaticism of it. The tenacity of it, leaching on to a religion, then seizing on ethnicity, race, community, a nation-state. There is the subtlety of it, its transmission through euphemisms and coda. Its positioning as the centerpiece of Nazism, the most devastating military-industrial machine ever assembled. There is even more than that.

All other forms of racism perceive the target group as inferior and treat them accordingly. Slavery, the reduction of humans to chattels, is based on the belief that superior races have the right to possess and exploit inferior ones. Colonialism, even practiced benevolently, is the product of a belief system that holds some races to be incapable of self-government. The exclusion of certain groups from professions, schools and social networks is derived from a feeling that members of that group would diminish those places.

The Jew is viewed entirely differently. He or she is not hated because of ignorant aversions to skin color or other physical attributes—such prejudices are so base and absurd that there is hope they can eventually be outgrown. The Jew is hated for something much more penetrating and elemental. The Jew is hated because of how he or she is perceived to think. This is not easily dislodged. The Jew is given a cunning malevolence, a capacity to trick and deceive. They are given a superior intellect but one that is perverse and drawn astray by dark forces. They use this intellect to plot the downfall of all non-Jews, to conspire to partake in their flesh, to murder their gods and prophets, to strip them of their wealth by the crafty accumulation of capital, to lead them into war, revolution and depression. No other ethnic group is subjected to such lurid formulations—accusations so wide and ludicrous no one could possibly rebut them.

No other victims of racism encounter greater denial of their plight. This inflicts a double indignity. Erasing the person, then denying that they had ever lived or died. Yes, Holocaust commemoration and education is now strongly embedded in the calendars and curricula of western nations. But this is as much a response to the ignorance and malice that accompanies the memory of the Holocaust than to the enormity of the event itself.

A poll conducted in the United States in 2020 found that a majority of Americans thought the number of Jews killed in the Holocaust was a third of the actual number. Nearly half were unable to name a single concentration or death camp. One in ten believed the Jews had caused the Holocaust.[8] The mere presence of deniers of the Holocaust, a meticulously

---

8   Kit Ramgopal, "Survey Finds 'Shocking' Lack of Holocaust Knowledge among Millennials and Gen Z," NBC News, September 16, 2020, https://www.nbcnews.com/news/world/survey-finds-shocking-lack-holocaust-knowledge-among-millennials-gen-z-n1240031.

documented event of recent history which spanned the European continent, continued for a period of five years, and involved millions of individual perpetrators, victims and witnesses, speaks to the grisly determination of the antisemite.

Of equal concern should be the more insidious, subtle and mainstream attempts to revise the history of the Holocaust through false equivalences, whereby every menace is a Nazi and every objectionable policy is a deportation to Auschwitz, every villain is a Goebbels or a Mengele, a phenomenon of soaring popularity among the pandemic conspiracy theorists. The attempts to reframe the Holocaust, and the Jews generally, to fit within modern theories of race further cloud our understanding of history and disfigures antisemitism into a lesser form of racism.

In January 2022, Whoopi Goldberg told an audience of millions on the show *The View* that the Holocaust "wasn't about race" on the basis that the Nazis and the Jews were "two groups of white people."[9] Goldberg, though surely through astonishing ignorance and not malice, excluded the Jews, who had been hunted and slaughtered precisely because of race, from being victims of the millions of racist crimes of which the Holocaust is formed. Kenneth L. Marcus referred to this as "erasive antisemitism," whereby the Jews are perceived only as being "white, privileged oppressors," and therefore incapable of being victims

---

9   James Hibberd, "Whoopi Goldberg Apologizes and Seemingly Doubles Down on Holocaust Comments," Hollywood Reporter, February 1, 2022, https://www.hollywoodreporter.com/tv/tv-news/whoopi-goldberg-the-view-holocaust-comment-draws-criticism-1235084661/.

of racism.[10] To arrive at such a view, one must first dabble in stereotypes of Jews as being wealthy, powerful and privileged.

The cases of the superstar recording artist Kanye West and basketball player Kyrie Irving demonstrate the enduring relevance of antisemitic mythology and the unparalleled opportunities for its distribution created by social media. The industrialist Henry Ford had to rely on writers and the printing press to spread his belief in a global Jewish conspiracy. Kanye West needed only to tap a few incendiary words on an iPhone to instantly reach many millions of people throughout the world. Pavel Krushevan used a St. Petersburg newspaper to introduce the world to *The Protocols of the Elders of Zion*. Now newspapers merely report on the immense damage Kyrie Irving caused entirely on his own.

Beginning in October 2022, Kanye West embarked on a prolonged, multimedia campaign ostensibly motivated by his belief that the Jews control the industries in which he attained his immense wealth and fame and were responsible for, among other things, exploiting Black entertainers. There was something deeply personal to the tenor of his statements, indicating it stemmed from some personal misfortune or slight he attributed to the collective Jew. Indeed, West accused the Jews of corrupting the Christian values of his former wife, Kim Kardashian, by advancing immoral content on major streaming services and other media.

---

10   David Bauder, "ABC Suspends Whoopi Goldberg over Holocaust Race Remarks," APNews, February 2, 2022, https://apnews.com/article/whoopi-goldberg-apology-the-holocaust-jonathan-greenblatt-4a4c77055d7bb1c37662fc9b274a8869.

When challenged for his statements, West claimed that he "actually can't be Anti Semitic [sic] because black people are actually Jew."

On October 14, 2022, West declared that when he awoke the following morning he would be "going death con 3 On JEWISH PEOPLE [sic]," a botched reference to the "DEFCON" state of readiness alerts used by the United States Armed Forces.

West then claimed Jews "black ball anyone who opposed their agenda," and were responsible for "cancel culture." Though initially dismissed as the ravings of someone laboring under a defect of mind, West's enormous wealth and cultural influence ensured that a sequence of long-form interviews across print, social media, network television and podcasts afforded him opportunity to fully ventilate his theories for a prolonged period to global audiences, virtually without challenge. Though ripe for mockery, virtually all that he said showed a certain lucidity, even a clarity of thought and purpose, that placed West comfortably alongside the antisemitic theorists and agitators that animate many of the chapters of this book.

In one segment, West told an interviewer that he was nearly poisoned by a Jewish doctor, immediately invoking recollections of the poisoners libel that emerged in the Middle Ages, and Stalin's "Doctors' Plot," in which Jewish doctors were accused of plotting to poison Communist Party figures. On a different occasion, West read out a graphic listing dozens of major media and entertainment companies before showing the supposedly Jewish executives highlighted in red,[11] giving

---

11 "Kanye West Shows Chart of Powerful Jews, Apologizes For George Floyd Comments, Talks MAGA Hat & More," published on YouTube

support for the concept that Jews have seized the levers of power and control every influential stratum, as foretold in the sequence of antisemitic texts that created the Jewish global domination myth.

In another interview, West claimed that "Jewish people have owned the Black voice…The Jewish community, especially in the music industry, in the entertainment [industry] period, they'll take one of us, the brightest of us, right, that can really feed a whole village, and they'll take us and milk us till we die."[12] This also invokes the global domination theme, and attributes a Jewish desire to enslave and kill, that came to be associated with the Blood Libel and Deicide charges. In yet another interview, with Chris Cuomo, he accused "Jewish record labels" of "modern-day slavery,"[13] showing the Jews had moved from oppressed to all-powerful oppressors and manipulating feelings in the African American community that the Jews were the cause of their misfortune.

West then told podcast host Lex Fridman that "there's a Jewish person right there controlling the country … controlling what the media says about me."[14] Referencing President Trump's son-in-law, West told the Drink Champs show, "Jared Kushner is an example of how the Jewish people have their hand on every single business that controls the world." West

---

by The Hollywood Fix, https://www.youtube.com/watch?v=P3MtX J00Jg4

12   Cited in "Kanye West: What You Need to Know," Anti-Defamation League, October 14, 2022, https://www.adl.org/resources/blog/ye-kanye-west-what-you-need-know.

13   Ibid.

14   Ibid.

also blamed Jews for propagating an immoral culture, leading his former wife, Kim Kardashian, to make personal sexual revelations, declaring that, "it's Jewish Zionists who are about that life, that's telling this Christian woman that has four black children to put that out as a message to the media."[15] West also said that "Kim has Zionist media handlers surrounding her."[16] West's accusations that Jews were purveyors of immorality and smut, and were destroying wholesome values of bygone eras, closely resembled the rhetoric of Henry Ford.

West's responses to criticism for his remarks and his abandonment by corporate sponsors and associates, a development he predictably blamed on the Jews also, illustrate the gaslighting, evasiveness and sheer duplicity that often accompany antisemitism. West fervently denied his antisemitism, but not on the basis that he harbored no ill-feeling towards Jews. Rather, he first claimed he could not be antisemitic, as he was himself a Jew—yet another conspiracy theory that holds Jews to be imposters who stole the identities of "real" Jews, African Americans. He then listed several Jews he was fond of in what is commonly known as the "some of my best friends are Jewish" defense. He then declared, "I'm starting to think anti Semitic [sic] means nigger," which flipped the tables on

---

15 Terry Zeller, "Kanye West Reacts to Kim Kardashian & Pete Davidson's 'Fireplace Sex' Story: Watch Kanye's Explosive Tirade on a Podcast Included Him Going Off on Kim and Pete Having Sex in Front of a Fireplace 'in honor of her grandmother,'" Hollywood Life, October 16, 2022, https://hollywoodlife.com/2022/10/16/kanye-west-reacts-kim-kardashian-pete-davidsons-fireplace-sex-video/.

16 Cited in "Kanye West: What You Need to Know," Anti-Defamation League, October 14, 2022, https://www.adl.org/resources/blog/ye-kanye-west-what-you-need-know.

his accusers, shifting the label of racist from himself, the perpetrator, to the people he had repeatedly denigrated for correctly identifying his attacks as antisemitic.

Kyrie Irving made social media posts about a book that advanced the "Jewish imposters" libel, and evaded direct questions from journalists calling on him to condemn antisemitism. Instead, Irving responded with, "I cannot be antisemitic if I know where I come from," a line he repeated twice, and which was widely interpreted to be a reinforcement of the African Americans are the authentic Jews fallacy, which is the subject of the book Irving initially promoted. Similarly, West posted, "you can't be anti-Semite when you know you are Semite."

Both men have brought previously fringe conspiracy theories to global attention, baited the Jewish world into what is perceived as a confrontation with Black America, and emboldened groups ranging from neo-Nazis to the Nation of Islam to escalate their own attacks on the Jews. Members of the extremist Goyim Defense League held a demonstration in Los Angeles displaying a banner over an Interstate that read "KANYE IS RIGHT ABOUT THE JEWS" while giving Nazi salutes. A Nation of Islam student minister endorsed West's comments, stating that Black people "are the real Semite, so to be antisemitic means to be anti-yourself." Another minister praised West for "speaking a lot of truth right now."

This book seeks to unpack all this and enable the reader to look through the euphemisms and hear the dog whistles through which antisemitism is expressed and transmitted. I have sought to take antisemitism to its very roots, investigate each myth and show where they come from, who created them, how they spread and what horrors have been inflicted in their name. I also explore whether these myths persist to this day, and if so, in what form. Do they motivate the shootings in synagogues, the beatings of Jews in the streets, the daubing of Jewish tombstones with the insignia of those who nearly wiped the Jews from the earth? Do they insinuate themselves, even subconsciously, in the extreme, often irrational rhetoric that animates so much of the discussion about anything Jewish?

Origins and evolution of antisemitism

The hatred of the Jews has long been rooted in psychology, a defect in reasoning projected outward. While the millennia have turned it into something reflexive or instinctive, a sense or urge rather than the result of a coherent thought-process, antisemitism began as something very deliberate, indeed rational. In its earliest forms, it arose from the unique circumstances in which the Jews placed themselves and were deliberately placed.

Religious tradition and historical evidence establish the Jews as a people indigenous to the Middle East. In a region of clans and tribes, they established their own tribe, then a sedentary society on the banks of the Mediterranean Sea probably after breaking away from Mesopotamia. Slavery in Egypt was unremarkable. The strong viewed the weak as economic resources. Egypt was strong. Israel was weak. Hence Israel was enslaved. The conquest of the Jewish kingdoms by Assyria, Babylon, Greece and Rome was predictable in an era of expansionistic empires. Israel was not a great empire hence it was conquered.

What is remarkable is that the ancient Jews survived as a distinct people, even became fortified in their sense of self, when others were simply washed away, absorbed into other nations and quickly disappeared. They emerged from slavery, they returned from Babylonian exile, they established their own little civilization with its distinct languages, cultural practices, connection to land and religious convictions.

When the great empires of the Greeks and Romans came upon the Jewish commonwealth, they sought to assimilate the Jews to spread their influence and suppress the independent thinking that is dangerous in a colonized people. The fact that the Jews refused to pray to foreign gods and waged heroic, often hopeless revolts, fearing not for any mortal rulers or generals, but their god alone, drove their conquerors to frenzy. Few are hated more than those who forget their lowly place.

They rebelled against Greek rule and won. They rebelled against Rome and were met with overwhelming force resulting in the destruction of their sacred temple, the renaming of their land from Judea to Palestina, mass slaughter, and expulsion of the remnants. The Emperor Hadrian despised the Jews and was intent on crushing this obstinate, upstart of a people who thought their belief in a single omnipotent God would see them outlive the glory of Rome.

The Jews were the first people to reject the worship of idols and many gods. Like all peoples, they tended to view their system of belief as enlightened and superior. It was certainly novel. It was, and remains, based on the worship of a single god who demands adherence to an exhaustive and rigid code of ethical, selfless living that sustains communities far better than military might. The Jews were naturally resented by those whose systems of belief they had witnessed and had rejected. Soon this idea of a society founded on ethical monotheism spread.

Both Christianity and Islam accepted the fundamental tenets of Judaism. But the successors could not live and thrive as mere sects or derivatives of Judaism.

In order to prove that their new faiths were the authentic word of God, they had to do one of two things: They could persuade the Jews, the original monotheists, to take on these new faiths and therefore admit that they were rightful successors or demonstrate that God's favor had passed to them by forcing the Jews into a permanently degraded state.

The eighth-century Muslim historian Ibn Ishaq wrote that Muhammad indeed asked the elders of the Jewish tribes who lived around him to adopt his new faith. In response, they "annoyed him with questions," testing his claims and propositions and finding them unconvincing.

This may well be history's earliest record of the Jews answering questions with questions. It also established the Jews as the villain in the story of Islam.

When the framers of these new faiths realized that the Jews would not be moved and stubbornly maintained that their conception of God, their prophets, their testament were complete and sufficient, they shifted to option two.

If the Jews weren't prepared to accept Christianity or Islam, they must be defeated and their existence must then evidence that defeat. How could the Jews claim to be correct in their beliefs if they lived in misery while Christians and Muslims thrived?

Mohammed vanquished the Jewish tribes after he had failed to persuade them. Early Christian leaders like John Chrysostom viciously sermonized against the Jews to bring about a hard and permanent split between Judaism and

Christianity. But he noticed that early Christians still dwelled in synagogues on the high holidays, drawn to the sound of the ram's horn and the familiarity of old customs.

Soon laws were enacted to isolate the Jews, bring them low, place them in perpetuity, in an excluded, humiliated state. If God hadn't vanquished the Jews, man would do his bidding and credit it to God anyway.

By this point, around the beginning of the Middle Ages, the fate of the Jews was essentially sealed. Suspicion descended on this oddity of a people who prayed in an extinct tongue and possessed no land, a stubborn relic clinging to ancient modes of worship like the drowning cling to reeds.

Wherever they went, they were followed by whispers of their misdeeds—there go the wandering and the wretched, the people who slew Christ, the tribe that poisoned Muhammad, what bestial thoughts lurk behind their dark and evasive eyes?

This in turn justified the enactment of more laws to prevent them from doing harm, resulting in further separation between Jews from non-Jews. In this separation, the suspicion and mythology around them grew.

Decrees forced Jews to be branded with distinct clothing, proclaimed that they could not appear in public during the Holy Week and could not hold public office. In the Islamic world, they were taxed heavily, and forbidden from walking on sidewalks in some countries. In Iran, Jews were forbidden from walking in the rain for fear that their uncleanliness would wash off to sully Muslim shoes.

The Council of Basel decreed in 1434 that Jews were forbidden from obtaining an academic degree and could not join Christians at festivities or banquets or engage "in much conversation." Jews were prohibited from joining guilds, thus excluding them from their traditional professions as merchants and craftsmen. This forced them more and more to turn to loathsome practices like moneylending, which forever bound up the Jews with the hated elements of interest and money and created a dangerous dynamic as Jewish subjects suddenly stood as creditor to their masters.

How could they pierce the growing body of suspicion and mythology that surrounded them if they had no power to speak to or engage with the people around them? This is why Jews cherish and defend their right to advocate to this day.

These cruel prohibitions made all the accusations about the Jews self-fulfilling. What was asserted about the Jews was made to come true. Of course, people thought them to be arrogant, aloof, tribal, backward and sinister because this assortment of laws that shut them in and shut them out, made them appear so.

These laws also established their inferiority, meaning that any citizen of a state no matter how low in status or oppressed could still take solace in being superior to any Jew. This was a necessary condition on the road to mob violence and eventual Nazi collaboration. It is also what turned any attempt by the Jews to improve their condition, any accomplishment collective or individual, into a source of mockery and contempt.

Then came global events and movements that had nothing to do with the Jews but would affect them profoundly. The spread of liberalism, the fall of old monarchies and power structures, the French and Russian Revolutions.

Napoleon tore down ghetto walls and revoked antisemitic laws in the territories he conquered. But this only ignited the fury of the local populations and fuelled theories spread by supporters of the old regimes that since the Jews had benefited from these revolutions, their dark hand had in fact orchestrated them.

This began an association of the Jew with modernity, radicalism and the destruction of traditional values and systems. The Jew became the symbol of everything good and cherished being swept away. This nostalgia for a purer, bygone age and the belief that the Jew is the agent of its pollution is something common to all antisemitic movements from Nazism to radical Islam.

With the decline of empires and the rise of national movements and nation-states based on ethnic, cultural, religious and linguistic cohesion, the Jews became a problem to be solved. Who were these people who as Leon Pinsker put it, "lived everywhere but nowhere in the right place"? They lived in their millions in Poland but were not Poles. In Germany but were not Germans. Amid the shifting borders and civil wars, the Jews became unwanted human stock that was very much in the way and could be set upon, ravaged and disposed of with impunity.

Then came the final disastrous evolution in human thinking. The advent of race science. The belief that the world is divided into distinct races, each with unchangeable, inherent physical and behavioural characteristics. Suddenly the Jewish problem could not be solved through conversion or assimilation, it required a "final solution."

As world war set in, the Jews could be robbed blind, herded into ghettoes, transported in cattle cars to purpose-built factories of mass death, gassed with a common pesticide or just shot into the Danube or crammed into barns and set alight, with virtually no opposition and with active support throughout

Europe. This was the endpoint of all the mythology and all the slander that had successfully branded this ancient people as vermin.

The creation of the modern State of Israel was meant to both end Jewish vulnerability and ameliorate antisemitism by placing the Jews on an equal footing to all other nations.

But Israel's experience has mirrored that of the Jew. In its early years, it attracted admiration for its pluckiness, its military feats against the marching armies of the Arab world. However, following its lightning victory in the 1967 War, Israel's success was perceived to have gone too far, becoming repellent to those who identify with the underdog or perhaps prefer a more docile, vulnerable specter of the Jew. It can be said that many have never forgiven Israel for daring to survive in 1967. Despite attaining full membership of the United Nations in 1949, Israel's place in the world is still contested, and it is frequently depicted as a unique force of evil.

The Holocaust should have completed the arc of antisemitism as the total and final fulfilment of every antisemitic fantasy in which any individual so inclined could freely partake. It ought to have shown that destroying the Jews means destroying ourselves. But the reservoir of defective reasoning and misdirected rage is self-replenishing. The same dogmas, the same crazy theories, the same willingness to believe, the same posing of Jewish questions persist. Are Jews nationalists or internationalists? Communists or capitalists? Do they control Hollywood? Should Israel exist? Are the Jews even Jews or are they an invented people? Can Jews understand British irony? Can Zionists be feminists? Did the Holocaust really happen?

The question of "why the Jews" remains ultimately unresolved and possibly unresolvable. It left its rational explanations long ago and now exists between the realms of psychology, history, religion and politics, which are incapable of producing a single, widely accepted proposition. But this book is less concerned with the "why" and more with the "how." At some point, the "why" ceases to be of paramount importance in actually confronting antisemitism. Why are the Jews hated? They simply are.

What is more critical is seeing "how" antisemitism is transmitted from generation to generation. How it takes hold in the hearts and minds of otherwise rational, decent people. How it degrades institutions, movements, nations and brings them to ruin. How it is used to incite murder. These are the questions that beg urgent answers. If we can understand "how," we can as individuals, communities and policy makers begin to take meaningful action.

The "how" is to be found in the conspiracy theories, the body of mythology that has clung to the Jews for millennia. Each antisemitic attack, each synagogue shooting can be attributed to one of the seven myths, or some alloy of them, that this book traces and reveals.

These deadly myths are nothing more than stories, vividly and repetitively told through art, propaganda posters, novels, plays and social media memes, to a willing audience. The power of storytelling, the capacity of fiction to arouse and inflame just as well as fact, is well understood.

In Primo Levi's *The Truce*, a memoir of his liberation from Auschwitz and journey back to his native Italy, Levi finds himself in a surreal transit camp in Russia. He observed how the

Russian soldiers reacted to the screening of third-rate films simply because they contained a clear hero versus villain narrative and an unambiguous moral proposition.

> It seemed as if the people in the film were not shadows to them, but flesh and blood friends or enemies, near at hand. The [hero] was acclaimed at every exploit, greeted by noisy cheers and sten-guns brandished perilously over their heads. The [villains] were insulted with bloodthirsty cries, greeted with shouts of "leave him alone," "go away," and "I'll get you," "kill them all." The audience stood up shouting, in generous defence of the innocent man; a wave of avengers moved threateningly towards the screen ... Stones, lumps of earth, splinters from the demolished doors, even a regulation boot flew against the screen, hurled with precision at the odious face of the great enemy.[17]

The medievalist historian Gavin Langmuir noted the effect of stories of the blood libel, the myth that brought to life the idea of Jewish bloodthirstiness. Langmuir called the record of the death of Little Hugh of Lincoln, supposedly through kidnapping, torture and crucifixion by an assembly of Jewish elders, "a vivid garbled yarn that would ring in men's minds for centuries ... and became a strand in English literature

---

17   Primo Levi, *The Truce* (New York: Hachette, 2019), 375.

and a support for irrational beliefs about Jews from 1255 to Auschwitz."[18]

Garbled maybe, but as British essayist Charles Lamb confessed, centuries later it still determined how he, an educated man, perceived the Jews. "I have not the nerve to enter one of their synagogues. Old prejudices cling about me. I cannot shake off the story of Little Hugh of Lincoln."[19]

Old prejudices are not easily unlearned. But it can be done. When we unravel these seven deadly myths, strip them down to their source, expose the dark, self-serving motives of those who advanced them, they lose their mystique and their hold over us. The myth of an all-powerful, all-controlling Jewish lobby will become less seductive if the stories and motives of Henry Ford and Hermann Goedsche are known and understood. The myth of the diabolical, child-killing Jew can finally dissipate if the stupidity and wickedness of its origin story is made plain. The weak of mind, the truly hateful will never be convinced by reason, but our aim should be to inoculate the wider public from these poisonous absurdities. If this is done, their ability to corrupt our reasoning and our perceptions falls away. The real Jew, flesh and blood, can then replace the mythical Jew in the world's consciousness.

It is in this spirit that this book has been written.

---

18 Gavin I. Langmuir, "The Knight's Tale of Young Hugh of Lincoln," *Speculum* 47, no. 3 (July 1972): 459–482.

19 Charles Lamb, *Imperfect Sympathies*, first published in *London Magazine*, August 1821, https://www.ourcivilisation.com/smart-board/shop/lamb/sympathy.htm.

A note about the Jewish people

The Jewish people today are an ethno-religious group with a global population of around 15 million. The two largest Jewish communities are in Israel (nearly 7 million) and the United States (around 6 million), with substantial communities of Jews (over 100,000) residing in Britain, France, Argentina, Russia, Canada, Germany and Australia.

Jewish law has traditionally defined a Jew according to matrilineal descent. In other words, if one's mother is a Jew, he or she is Jewish. However, personal identification with the Jewish people is in reality much broader and looser, encompassing those of patrilineal Jewish descent and converts to Judaism.

The Jews became a cohesive, national group in lands approximating the current territories of the State of Israel, the Palestinian Territories (variously referred to as the West Bank, Palestine and Judea & Samaria), Jordan and parts of Syria, Lebanon and Egypt.

The existence of a sedentary socio-economic group bound by language, custom, method of worship and tribal affiliations is evidenced by archaeological discoveries and historical sources. The existence of a people and a society known as "Israel" can be traced more than 3,200 years to the dawn of the Iron Age. The oldest reference to a people called "Israel" is to be found on a stone monument of the Egyptian Pharaoh Merenptah, son of Rameses. There it is proclaimed: "Israel is laid waste, his seed is not."

Historians have noted that as early as the thirteenth century BCE, "Israel" referred to a socio-ethnic entity which consisted of a sedentary, agricultural society. The same people were earlier referred to as Hebrews (derived from the Mesopotamian, "Habiru"), and following the destruction of the northern Jewish kingdom of Israel by Assyria in 722 BCE and the survival of the southern kingdom of Judea, the people came to be known as Jews (from Judeans). Judea was colonized and then destroyed by Rome following failed Jewish revolts in 70 CE and 135 CE.

While a sizeable Jewish diaspora had existed since 587 BCE following the exile of Jewish nobles by Babylon, the defeats by Rome resulted in the comprehensive dispersal of the people throughout the Roman Empire. This dispersal created three primary sub-groups of the Jewish people: *Ashkenazi*, being those Jews who settled in Germany and tended to move east-ward into Poland and Russia; *Sephardi*, being Jews who settled in Spain and from there moved to the Americas, Turkey, North Africa; and the *Mizrachi*, those Jews who settled in the Arabian Peninsula, Iran, Syria, Lebanon and remained in the former territories of the Jewish homeland, which by decree of the Roman Emperor Hadrian following the expulsion of 135 CE had come to be known as Palestine.

Jewish religious affiliation is characterized by different streams ranging from ultra-orthodox to reform and recon-structionist. As Jews possess not only common religious practices but culinary, linguistic, literary and other cultural, national and biological commonalities, the complete absence of religious observance does not negate Jewish identity.

While Jewish law considers Jewish status to be irrevocable except in isolated cases of excommunication, in practice, peo-ple cease to affiliate or be seen to affiliate to the Jewish people by virtue of converting to another faith or through a loss of identity or connection.

A note about the term "antisemitism"

The term "antisemitism" is a modern creation and a wholly unsatisfactory one. The word was created by a German populist and agitator, Wilhelm Marr, in 1879 to give anti-Jewish activities a legitimacy and a sound of pseudo-scientific sophistication. Marr founded the League of Antisemites. It is often and incorrectly spelled with a hyphen and capitalization of "semitism" (anti-Semitism), which falsely suggests a hatred of Semites or Semitism. No such people exist, though the word "Semitic" refers to a linguistic family which includes Arabic and Hebrew. This has led to claims that antisemitism refers to hatred of both Jews and Arabs when in fact the term was created by Marr only with hatred of the Jews in mind. As in the cases of Kanye West and basketballer Kyrie Irving, self-identifying as a "Semite" has become a way of denying being antisemitic despite making remarks hateful towards Jews.

While most scholars and commentators agree that the term "antisemitism" itself confuses the subject it seeks to describe, there is no consensus on a better alternative. Other formulations such as Judeophobia, Jew-hatred and anti-Jewish racism aren't as expansive as "antisemitism" insofar as they do not capture the religious, racial and national expressions of antisemitism, but at least they make clear what the term means and who the subject is. However, as "antisemitism" is the dominant term to describe hatred of Jews, it is used throughout this book.

While numerous scholarly and working definitions of it have been developed and applied, in its essence antisemitism is a hatred of the Jews, which has been expressed variously as a hatred for the Jewish religion, and hatred of Jews as members of an ethnic, national and perceived racial group.

It should be noted that antisemitism is often expressed through the use of euphemism or coded language which deliberately avoids the use of the term "Jew" in order to elude accusations of racism and to bolster the appeal of this form of prejudice. The term "antisemitism" is itself an example of such obfuscation. Zionism, which refers to the political/national movement to re-establish an independent Jewish homeland in Palestine is the most commonly used euphemism in contemporary antisemitic speech.

While sometimes used to express opposition to the process by which the modern State of Israel was created or opposition to policies emanating from its government, it is also used to convey a hatred of the Jews while allowing the user to mendaciously claim they are merely engaging in political critiques. The use of terms such as "Zionist Occupied Government" by American white nationalist groups and the proliferation of classically antisemitic texts in the Soviet Union from the 1950s, which substituted "Jew" with "Zionist" to avoid condemnation for racism, are the most striking examples of this process. Regard must be had to the substance of what is said and not merely the form, which can be duplicitous. The use of traditionally antisemitic motifs or claims, including global domination, control of government and media, bloodlust, obsession with money, when levelled against Jewish individuals or collectives, are to be regarded as antisemitic whether the word "Jew" is used or not. To do otherwise would be to give benefit of doubt where none exists.

MYTH 1

The Blood Libel

———

Rendering of a blood libel. Rijksmuseum, CC0, via Wikimedia Commons

> "Every seven years the Jews catch a stranger,
> whom they offer as a sacrifice, tearing his flesh into shreds."[1]
> —Democritus

On March 23, 1475, in the Alpine town of Trent, in what was then Austria and is now Italy, two-year-old boy Simon Unferdoren disappeared. A canal ran alongside the boy's home and Simon's father feared that his son had fallen into it and drowned. The following morning, on Good Friday, the boy's father reported the disappearance to Bishop Hinderbach, who governed Trent under authority of the Holy Roman Emperor Frederick III. Hinderbach ordered his chief magistrate to conduct a search, which proved fruitless. As the hours passed with no trace of the boy, suspicion fell on the few Jewish families who lived in Trent. Rumors spread that Jews murdered Christian children during the festival of Passover in a re-enactment of the torment and death of Christ. Passover and Easter fell on the same days in that year heightening religious fervor. A search party was dispatched to the substantial property of a local Jew named Samuel. No evidence of the boy's presence or of any crime was detected.

On the evening of March 26, a Jewish servant of Samuel's discovered the body of Simon in a canal that ran under Samuel's house. The discovery was immediately reported to the authorities. Simon's body was then examined by physicians including the private physician of Bishop Hinderbach,

---

1 Quoted in H. L. Strack, "Blood Accusation," *The Jewish Encyclopaedia*, vol. 3 (New York and London, 1902), 260.

a man known as Tiberino. The heads of each Jewish family in Trent were arrested.

On April 4, 1475, Tiberino travelled to his hometown of Brescia in the northern Italian region of Lombardy to inform the Senate of the death of Simon of Trent. The Jews of Trent had been rounded up and awaited trial. They steadfastly maintained their innocence.

Tiberino declared before the Senate that he intended to spread the story of Simon so that Jews "may be eliminated from the whole Christian world" and the memory of them "utterly vanish from the land of the living."[2] In the coming weeks, confessions from the Jews were taken under intense and prolonged torture. One Jew, a traveller passing through Trent, beseeched his interrogators, "tell me what you want me to say, and I will say it."[3]

Tiberino told the Senate that the Jews had met in secret and decided to take the blood of a Christian child to mask the "powerful stench" given off by the unleavened bread known as Matzo that Jews bake on Passover to remember their hurried escape from bondage in Egypt. One of the Jews was then assigned the task of abducting a Christian child, whereupon Simon was identified, lured and pacified with a silver coin. He was then subjected to excruciating torture including "tearing apart his right jaw next to his chin," the "piercing of the boy's penis," stabbing the boy with "hard needles" to release his blood, and ripping off flesh from the boy's inner thigh.

---

2   Quoted in Magda Teter, *Blood Libel: On the Trail of an Antisemitic Myth* (Cambridge, MA: Harvard University Press, 2020), 47.

3   Ibid., 56.

To establish the guilt of each of Trent's Jewish families, Tiberino asserted that each Jewish participant had taken a turn "cutting for himself a little bit of the living flesh." All the while, Simon remained alive to take the taunts of the Jews which Tiberino insisted included, "let us butcher this boy just like Jesus, the Christian's God, who is nothing."[4]

Tiberino concluded with an impassioned cry for the expulsion of the Jews. "Listen, you rulers of peoples, to the unheard-of-crime and watch over your peoples as faithful shepherds should! Let earth's denizens awake and see what snakes they are nurturing in their own bosom! The cruel Jews not only eat up Christian's property in their frenzied craving for interest payments, but, conspiring against our lives and destruction, they feast on the blood of our sons, afflicting them with terrible punishments in their synagogues and cruelly slaughtering them in place of Christ."[5]

But as the weeks passed and the Jews continued to wallow in the town prison, scepticism set in about whether these Jewish families had indeed carried out the outrageous acts of which they were accused. The Vatican was concerned that blood libel accusations would destabilize the Church and the new miracles that were being attributed to Simon each day would reduce the Church to a cult.

Various explanations were offered for why the Jews of Trent would have carried out such an abominable crime and in such a fantastical way, including that Jews used Christian blood to reverse Jewish male menstruation. Others asserted that the

4   Ibid., 48.
5   Ibid., 49.

Jewish rejection of Jesus as the son of God necessitated the murder of non-Jewish children.[6]

A common feature of blood libel cases is the role of a single initiator, invariably a man of high office, good standing and sound education, often driven by motives such as financial indebtedness, who manipulates the passions of the many to satisfy some visceral desire to see the Jews humiliated, defeated and removed. In the case of Simon of Trent, that man was Bishop Hinderbach.

As the trial proceeded, new accounts of miracles were attributed to Simon. The town became a pilgrimage site for Christian worshippers and Bishop Hinderbach sought the canonization of Simon by Pope Sixtus IV. The juxtaposition of Simon's gruesome death with his rising godliness further enhanced the magnitude of the crime attributed to the Jews. Hinderbach then commissioned poets, writers and artists to produce graphic accounts of the torture and death of Simon, which were disseminated throughout the continent.

The culmination of all this was that fifteen Jewish men of Trent were burned alive in a public execution. The story of Simon of Trent spread across Europe, aided by the hagiographic depictions of Simon and the shocking accounts of the crime. Mob violence was inflicted on Jews in nearby towns and the Jews of Vicenza were expelled in 1486.[7]

The disappearance or death of any child now immediately thrust suspicion on the members of the peculiar, secluded

---

6   Ibid., 81.
7   R. Po-Chia Hsia, *Trent 1475: Stories of a Ritual Murder Trial* (New Haven: Yale University Press, 1992).

nation in their midst. Geoffrey Chaucer's *The Prioress's Tale*, which depicted the Jewish ritual murder of a Christian child, further seared the characterization into the collective psyche. The German historian Johann Christoph Wagenseil observed that "because of those damned lies the Jews have been plagued, tormented, and many thousands of them cruelly executed."[8]

The blood libel may have been "one of the most bizarre and dangerous legends ever created by the human imagination,"[9] yet its imagery was simply too potent and too severe to dislodge, particularly in an age of irrationalism.

In 1840, following a blood libel case in Damascus, Syria, the Sultan Abdul Mejid ordered an investigation of the accusations and issued a proclamation of the findings.

> An ancient prejudice prevailed against the Jews. The ignorant believed that the Jews were accustomed to sacrifice a human being, to make use of his blood at their feast of Passover ... The religious books of the Hebrews have been examined by learned men, well versed in their religious literature, the result of which examination is that it is found that Jews are strongly prohibited not only from using human blood but even that of animals. It therefore follows

---

8   Teter, *Blood Libel*, 178.
9   "The Ritual Murder or Blood Libel Legend: A Study of Anti-Semitic Victimization through Projective Inversion," In *Meaning of Folklore: The Analytical Essays of Alan Dundes*, ed. Simon Bronner J., (Logan, UT: University Press of Colorado, 2007), 382.

> that the charges made against them and their
> religion are nothing but pure calumnies ...
> we cannot permit the Jewish nation whose
> innocence of the crime alleged against them is
> evident to be vexed and tormented upon accu-
> sations which have not the least foundation in
> truth.[10]

But the Sultan's rational observations were no match for the chilling stories of abduction, the gory details of snarling Jews pricking, taunting and hacking helpless children, with the added infusion of mock crucifixion to harden Christian outrage.

The Nazis grasped the power of this mythology. In May 1943, the head of the Nazi SS Heinrich Himmler wrote to the Chief of Police in Berlin, Ernst Kaltenbrunner, "we should proceed to investigate ritual murders among the Jews ... I have the idea that we could pass on these ritual murder cases to the press in order to facilitate the evacuation of Jews from these countries. In short, I am of the opinion that we could give anti-semitism an incredible virulence with the help of antisemitic propaganda by giving huge publicity to ritual murders."[11]

In the same year, the Nazis published a book titled *Jewish Ritual Murder*, which catalogued blood libel accusations throughout history. The Nazi newspaper *Der Sturmer* published a "blood libel" edition bearing the cover artwork of Jews collecting Christian blood. A children's book titled *The Poisonous*

---

10   Ibid., note 31.
11   Ibid., note 60.

Mushroom, depicting the Jews as killers and torturers of children, was also published.

Historian Salomon Reinach observed: "Of all the accusations which fanaticism and ignorance have used as a weapon against Judaism, there is none which can be compared in terms of improbability and absurdity to that of ritual murder."[12] The blood libel has proven so impervious to logic because it is an unforgettable cautionary tale, a spook story to distrust the stranger, and to fear those whose beliefs and rituals are unfamiliar. It also appeals to our biological instinct to protect and avenge the child.

For the most part, accusations of Jews stealing children for the purpose of ritual murder have receded into the annals of absurdity. However, as historian Magda Teter notes, "the blood libel survives—adapting to changing and political climates."[13] Indeed, the blood libel has "enjoyed the hardiest tenacity"[14] of all antisemitic myths. The depiction of conspiring, vengeful Jews revelling in the blood of the weak and innocent remains a fixture of modern antisemitic discourse. It has primed society to believe that the Jews are capable of the most merciless conduct, operating outside the bounds of humanity.

In May 2021, commenting on an escalation in the Israeli-Palestinian conflict, Turkish President Recep Tayyip Erdogan

---

12   Ibid.
13   Teter, *Blood Libel*, 2.
14   Joshua Trachtenberg, *The Devil and the Jews: The Medieval Conception of the Jew and its Relation to Modern Antisemitism* (New Haven: Yale University Press, 1943), quoted in Alan Dundes, *The Blood Libel Legend: A Casebook in Antisemitic Folklore* (Madison: University of Wisconsin Press, 1991), 337.

declared, "it is in their nature. They are murderers, to the point that they will kill children who are five or six years old. They only are satisfied by sucking their blood."[15]

Others seek no cover in political language or euphemism and see the original blood libel as the true rendering of the Jew. On April 28, 2019, on the last day of the festival of Passover, a nineteen-year-old man, John T. Earnest, entered the Chabad of Poway synagogue, just north of San Diego. Earnest opened fire with a semi-automatic rifle killing a sixty-year-old woman and wounding three other worshippers. Before carrying out the shooting, Earnest had uploaded his manifesto to the unregulated message board 8chan. Within it, Earnest had written, "You are not forgotten Simon of Trent, the horror that you and countless children have endured at the hands of the Jews will never be forgiven."[16]

---

15 Laura Kelly, "US Condemns Erdoğan Comments as Antisemitic," Hill, May 19, 2021, https://thehill.com/policy/national-security/554277-us-condemns-erdogan-comments-as-antisemitic.

16 Teter, Blood Libel, 2 note 8.

MYTH 2

Christi-Killers

Christ bound and beaten by Jews. Etching by Heinrich Nüsser after
J. F. Overbeck, 1850, https://creativecommons.org/licenses/by/4.0,
via Wikimedia Commons

> "He is son, in that he is begotten.
> He is sheep, in that he suffers.
> He is human, in that he is buried.
> He is God, in that he is raised up.
> This is Jesus the Christ, to whom be
> the glory for ever and ever …
> "It is he that has been murdered
> And where has he been murdered?
> In the middle of Jerusalem
> By whom? By Israel."[1]
> Melito of Sardis, *On Pascha*, circa 190 CE

The Christ-killers libel holds the Jews both collectively and perpetually guilty for the death of Jesus. It is the supreme charge. Deicide, literally the killing of a god, enabled a permanent severing of Christianity from the Jewish faith from which it stemmed and established the Jews as the supreme villains in the arc of Christian history, a satanic presence in the realm of the Lord.

This conception of the Jews is derived from accounts of the arrest and death of Jesus written by his disciples.

Much of Jesus's life and death two thousand years ago remains unknowable and therefore intensely contested. What is known is that Jesus was a Jew both by birth and by self-identification. He lived in what was the Jewish homeland, Judea, which fell under Roman occupation for nearly four hundred years beginning in 63 BCE. Pope Benedict, in his book *Jesus of Nazareth*, wrote "Jesus and all his followers were ethnically

---

1   Melito of Sardis, *On Pascha* (Crestwood, NY: St. Vladimir's Seminary Press, 2001), 56–57.

Jews. The entire early Christian community was made up of Jews."[2] We know also that Jesus preached within a Jewish society that he was seeking to influence and reform. As New Testament scholars Spivey and Smith noted, "the earliest Christians did not think of themselves as members of a new religion separate from Judaism,"[3] nor did they seek to break away from Judaism and found a new faith. As is ascribed to Jesus in the Gospel of Matthew: "Think not that I have come to abolish the law and the prophets; I have come not to abolish them but to fulfill them."[4]

Claims that Jesus was the Messiah foretold in Jewish prophecy would no doubt have been viewed as a threat to the power structures within Jewish society. Rome had turned Judea into a vassal and had no tolerance for Jews claiming to be divine and therefore superior to the emperors of Rome. By all accounts, the Roman governor of Judea Pontius Pilate was cruel and vindictive, and under his authority Jews were routinely condemned to the torturous mode of public execution known as crucifixion.

Did the Jewish leadership vigorously demand the execution of Jesus for his preaching, even coercing Pontius to this end? Was the Jewish population supportive of the execution? Were they divided, indifferent or even widely unaware? Did Pontius suffer bouts of angst and uncertainty over the death of Jesus,

---

2   Philip Pullella, "Pope Book Says Jews not Guilty of Jesus Christ's Death," Reuters, March 3, 2011, https://www.reuters.com/article/us-pope-jews-idUSTRE7216Y720110302.

3   R. A. Spivey and D. M. Smith, *Anatomy of the New Testament*, 3rd ed. (New York: Fortress Press, 1982), 13.

4   Gospel according to Matthew 5:17.

ultimately washing his hands of the matter and shifting moral responsibility onto the Jews? Were the Jews so determined to see Jesus killed that they chanted their wilful acceptance of eternal responsibility for all to hear and one to record?

These are the questions that cannot be definitively answered and thus became susceptible to creative interpretation often with a clear political or malicious purpose.

Within this ambiguity arose a distinct narrative, one which established the divinity of Jesus, the innocence of Rome and the eternal guilt of the Jews.

The canonical Gospels (the "good news") are four accounts of the words and deeds of Jesus, written by Matthew, Luke, John and Mark between the years 70 and 95 CE.

As we see from the Gospel of John, the aim of these writings was not to record a historical account of Jesus's life and death but to sway audiences to the new faith: "These things are written that you may believe that Jesus is the Messiah, the Son of God."[5]

While Jesus and his disciples sought to influence and reform the Jewish society of which they were a part, the Gospels, written decades later, intended for the teachings of Jesus to form the basis for a new monotheistic faith, that ultimately displaced Judaism. This required the characterization of Jesus and his Jewish followers as fundamentally and irreconcilably distinct from the Jews, otherwise believers could straddle both faiths or move between them.

---

5   Jeremy Cohen, *Christ Killers: The Jews and the Passion from the Bible to the Big Screen* (New York: Oxford University Press, 2007), 16.

This was achieved in part by Jesus's followers abandoning Jewish traditions, including circumcision of new-born males, strict dietary laws and the observance of the Sabbath. More profoundly, this was achieved by placing the rejection, betrayal and torture of Jesus at the feet of the rival faith.

It was the fourth and final Gospel, the Gospel of John, which most distinctly established the Jews as the villain in the Jesus story, shifting responsibility from the Romans who the new Christians were seeking to placate, and laying it squarely upon the politically powerless Jews from whom they were seeking to separate.

In the first three Gospels, the usage "the Jews" occurs a total of eighteen times. In John, it is used seventy-one times. The Five Books of Moses (the Torah or Old Testament) which Jesus himself had preached, are referred to in John as "their laws."[6] The Jews are referred to as the offspring of the devil.[7]

A straight reading of John left no doubt as to collective Jewish guilt. Try as modern theologians might to interpret "the Jews" to mean "some Jews" or "Jewish leaders," to the devoted throughout history, John made plain that the Jews, all Jews, were the murderers of their God.

"And therefore did the Jews persecute Jesus, and sought to slay him." (5:16)

"The Jews sought the more to kill him, because he not only had broken the sabbath, but said also that God was his Father." (5:18)

"Then the Jews took up stones again to stone him." (10:31)

---

6   Gospel according to John 15:25.
7   Ibid., 8:44.

"The officers of the Jews seized Jesus and bound him." (18:12)

"The Jews answered him, "We have a law, and by that law he ought to die." (19:7)

As the Protestant scholar Eldon Jay Eppmore wrote, "more than any other book in the canonical body of Christian writings, John is responsible for the frequent antisemitic expressions by Christians during the past eighteen or nineteen centuries, and particularly for the unfortunate and still existent characterization of the Jewish people by some Christians as 'Christ-killers.'"[8]

While John is widely regarded as the originator of Christian antisemitism, it can be argued that the Gospel of Matthew inflicted more misery than the rest of Christian liturgy combined. In nine words, which together came to be known as "the blood curse," Matthew established that the Jews freely accepted their guilt for the murder of Jesus, now and forever.

As Pilate washed his hands before the Jewish crowd and declared himself "innocent of this man's blood," Matthew records that the Jewish crowd replied, "His blood be upon us and upon our children."[9]

The words appeared in no other Gospel and there is no custom in the Jewish faith of binding one's children in an oath, not least such an oath. Yet these nine words effectively fixed the Jews in a distinct role in the story of Christianity as the

8   D. Moody Smith, "Judaism and the Gospel of John," in *Jews and Christians: Exploring the Past, Present, and Future*, ed. James H. Charlesworth (New York: Crossroad, 1990), 76–96.

9   Gospel according to Matthew 27:24–25.

new faith spread thought the Roman Empire. The words taught Christians to hate the Jews,[10] and to see the Jews not as the progenitors of their own beliefs and the source of their own scriptures but as a plainly cursed people destined to suffer for all time and for whom no punishment would be excessive.

The blood curse had a deeply practical purpose. It carved out a Christian identity as members of a new and distinct faith and effected a "parting of ways" between Matthew's Christian community and the synagogue across the street.[11]

It also steeped the Jews in a villainy they would never fully escape. Pope Innocent III summed it up in this way: "Christian piety accept the Jews who, by their own guilt, are consigned to perpetual slavery because they crucified the Lord."[12] As Peter the Venerable put it, God wishes for them "a life worse than death."[13]

The telling of the suffering and death of Christ at the hands of the perfidious Jews who beheld the Lord and slew him, was the foundation story of Christianity. As such, as the faith spread, the Christ-killers libel spread with it.

The still-used service of the Twelve Passion Gospels on Thursday Evening, Eastern Orthodox Church declares: "Jews sought to kill You, O Lord, with thirty pieces of silver and a deceitful kiss … Today, Jews had the Lord nailed to the Cross,

---

10 Lloyd Gaston, "The Messiah of Israel as Teacher of the Gentiles: The Setting of Matthew's Christology," *Interpretation* 29, no. 1 (January 1975): 24–40.

11 Graham N. Stanton, "The Gospel of Matthew and Judaism," Manson Memorial Lecture delivered in the University of Manchester on November 3, 1983.

12 Cohen, *Christ Killers*, 87.

13 Ibid., 123.

the Lord who parted the sea with the rod and led them in the wilderness. Today, they had His side pierced with the spear, who for their sake had smitten Egypt with plagues ... That swarm of murderers of God, that gathering of Jews who defied the Law."[14]

The glorious art of Caravaggio, Velazquez and Raphael vividly depicted the crucifixion, others painted his betrayal by Judas, his mockery at the hands of the Jews and his crowning with thorns, flagellation and other inflictions of torture. Passion plays re-enacting the death of Christ, often with gruesome embellishment, became annual traditions. The faithful were urged to "take up the cross" by Pope Urban II and the Crusaders took to marking the cross on their garments.[15]

The Crusades, beginning in 1096, saw the faithful set out from Europe on expeditions to liberate the Holy Land from Islamic rule. As they journeyed, the Crusaders became conscious of the Jewish communities situated along their path. "What is the good of going to the end of the world, at great loss of men and money, when we permit among us other infidels a thousand times more guilty towards Christ than the Mohammedans?"[16] The Jews were beset by the Crusaders and were offered conversion or death. The massacres began in Rouen, France and quickly spread to the Rhineland, where they were most brutal and unsparing. By the time the Crusaders were finished with them, the Jewish communities

---

14   Antiphon 5, Antiphon 6, service of the Twelve Passion Gospels on Thursday Evening, Eastern Orthodox Church, https://www.annunciationorthodox.org/assets/files/thursday-evening-text.pdf.

15   Cohen, *Christ Killers*, 119.

16   Dennis Prager and Joseph Telushkin, *Why the Jews: The Reason for Antisemitism* (Denver: Touchstone, 2007), 81.

there were completely destroyed. Promises of protection by local bishops and lords were either withdrawn or proved futile in the face of the mob. The massacres "set a disastrous precedent, depositing a fatal poison in the European psyche and imagination."[17]

In addition to being used to justify an expansive body of anti-Jewish ordinances, violence and expulsion, the accusation of deicide brought forth a series of secondary libels that were no less disastrous. It could not be otherwise. If the Jews were condemned as the people "who killed both the Lord Jesus and the prophets,"[18] as Paul put it in his First Letter to the Thessalonians, they were surely capable of anything.

The myth of Jewish ritual murder (discussed in Myth 1) was an outgrowth of the Christ-killers myth. It contained the same powerful motifs of sadism, conspiracy and bloodlust. It was founded on a narrative that the Jews, who had suffered persecution as divine punishment for their crime of crimes, grew ever more vengeful, and so conspired to take Christian children to re-enact the crucifixion.

The Christ-killers libel also established the Jews as seeking the destruction of Christianity and Christians.[19] In the face of this, attacks on the Jews could be rationalized as acts of

17 D. Nirenberg, "The Rhineland Massacres of Jews in the First Crusade: Memories Medieval and Modern," in *Medieval Concepts of the Past: Ritual, Memory, Historiography*, ed. G. Althoff, J. Fried, and P. Geary (Cambridge: Cambridge University Press, 2002), 279–310.

18 First Epistle to the Thessalonians 2:14–15.

19 Samuel K. Cohn, "The Black Death and the Burning of Jews," *Past & Present* 196 (2007): 13.

necessity and self-defense. Martin Luther had said of the Jews, "if they could kill us all, they would gladly do so."[20]

The libel of Jews as poisoners developed through this reasoning. As Europe succumbed to the Black Death and struggled to comprehend why such disaster had befallen the Christian world, suspicion naturally fell on the Jewish communities in their midst.

The Jews had already been forcibly separated from their non-Jewish neighbors through Church decrees that limited interactions between Jews and Christians and regulated where Jews could live and work. This created a permanent state of hostility and distrust. Now, rumors circulated that the Jews weren't dying from the plague like everyone else. This was an outright lie that would be mirrored centuries later by claims that no Jews had died in the World Trade Center attacks (around three hundred did[21]) and that four thousand Jews with advance knowledge of the attacks had coordinated to take the day off.[22]

In fact, Jewish communities in Europe were ravaged by the Black Death like everybody else despite the observance of laws that probably made transmission less likely, including the immediate burial of the dead and ritual handwashing before meals.

---

20 Prager and Telushkin, *Why the Jews*, 85.
21 Adam Kirsch, "No Escape," Tablet Magazine, September 6, 2011, https://www.tabletmag.com/sections/arts-letters/articles/no-escape.
22 Linda Grant, "The Hate that Will not Die," *Guardian,* December 18, 2001, https://www.theguardian.com/world/2001/dec/18/september 11.israel.

Amid the biblical calamity of plague, rumors quickly spread accusing the Jews of conspiring to murder their Christian neighbors just as they had done to Jesus.

"The Jews wished to extinguish all of Christendom, through their poisons of frogs and spiders mixed into oil and cheese,"[23] was how one writer put it.

In Basel, on January 9, 1349, six hundred Jews were burned alive on a sandbank of the Rhine. Their children were snatched away and forcibly baptized.[24]

In Winterthur and Diessenhoven, local rulers demanded the execution of the Jews despite the objections of the duke. The duke eventually wilted and ordered the mass burnings of Jews within his jurisdiction.[25]

In Strasbourg, two thousand Jews were burned on row stakes.[26] Emperor Charles IV of Bohemia made arrangements for the seizure of Jewish property and coordinated the execution of the Jews of Nuremberg, Regensburg, Augsburg and Frankfurt.[27]

---

23 7 Die Weltchronik des Monchs Albert, 1273177'- 1454/56, ed. Rolf Sprandel (MGH, Scriptores rerum Germanicarum in usum scholarum, new ser., xvii, Munich, 1994), 109.

24 Alfred Haverkamp, "'Conflitti interni" e collegamenti sovralocali nelle città tedesche durante la prima metà del XTV secolo," in *Annali dell Istituto storico italo-germanico* 13 (1984): *Aristocrazia cittadina e ceti popolari nel tardo Medioevo in Italia e in Germania*, ed. Reinhard Elze and Gina Fasoli, 162; Germania Judaica, ed. Avneri, ii, 53.

25 Cohn, "The Black Death and the Burning of Jews," 19.

26 B. W. Tuchman, *A Distant Mirror: The Calamitous 14th Century* (New York: Ballantine Books, 1972).

27 Joshua Trachtenberg, *The Devil and the Jews: The Medieval Conception of the Jew and its Relation to Modern Antisemitism* (1943), 2nd ed. (Philadelphia, 1983), 105.

A chaplain to Pope John XXII, Heinrich Truchess von Diessenhoven, was moved to praise the Almighty for the annihilation of the Jews: "And blessed be God who confounded the ungodly who were plotting the extinction of his church."[28] Von Diessenhoven observed that those who managed to escape the infernos were greeted by men wielding "cudgels and stones" who "dashed out the brains of those trying to creep out of the fire."[29] "Within one year," he noted, "all the Jews between Cologne and Austria were burnt," "and in Austria they await the same fate, for they are the accursed of God."[30]

In January 1406, the Jews were expelled from Florence on the basis that "the killers of Christ were 'polluting' the countryside."[31]

The mass killings of Jews during the Black Death continued the rhythm set during the Crusades and that would reside with the peoples of Europe until the Holocaust. Codes of law and societal norms could simply be set aside and the killers of Christ, who had "disowned themselves of God's favour"[32] could be dispossessed, brutalized and slayed.

The depiction of the Jews as poisoners experienced a resurgence during the COVID-19 pandemic. Turkish state television aired a segment during which a guest claimed that "Jews,

---

28 Rosemary Horrox, ed., *The Black Death* (Manchester: Manchester University Press, 1994), 208.

29 Dan Freedman, "Why Were Jews Blamed for the Black Death?," Moment Magazine, https://momentmag.com/why-were-jews-blamed-for-the-black-death/.

30 Ibid.

31 Cohn, "The Black Death and the Burning of Jews," 23.

32 Cohen, *Christ Killers*, 31.

Zionists, have organized and engineered the novel coronavirus as a biological weapon just like the bird flu 'to design the world, seize countries, and neuter the world's population.'"[33] In monitoring far-right social media and chat forums, the Anti-Defamation League identified a recurring theme that COVID was a "calculated, long-term Jewish plot to institute 'Global Jew Government,'" a modern mutation of the blood libel and global domination myths.[34]

It took centuries of carnage committed in the name of the Church to prompt deep reflection on just what was being done to the Jews in the name of the Christian faith.

"The planned and rationalised murder of circa 6,000,000 Jews, committed by baptized Christians in the heart of Christendom,"[35] could not be ignored. There began a careful process of interpreting the Gospels so as to maintain their integrity while rejecting the myth of Jewish collective guilt.

Pope Benedict asserted that an analysis of the Gospels indicates that the arrest and execution of Jesus was pursued by "Temple aristocracy," who wanted Jesus condemned to death because he had declared himself king of the Jews and had, in doing so, blasphemed and violated Jewish religious law.[36]

The landmark proclamation of Pope Paul VI in 1965, known as "Nostra Aetate," saw the official rejection by the Church of

---

33 Manfred Gerstenfeld, "Anti-Jewish Coronavirus Conspiracy Theories in Historical Context," in *The COVID-19 Crisis: Impact and Implications*, ed. Efraim Kars (Ramat Gan: Begin-Sadat Center for Strategic Studies, 2020), http://www.jstor.org/stable/resrep26356.12.

34 Naomi Levin, "Hate Wave," *Australia/Israel Review*, July 26, 2021.

35 Cohen, *Christ Killers*, 170.

36 Philip Pullella, "Pope Book Says Jews not Guilty of Jesus Christ's Death".

the Christ-killers libel. "What happened in His passion," it pronounced, "cannot be charged against all the Jews, without distinction, then alive, nor against the Jews of today."[37] The spirit of conciliation in the papal decrees has for the most part been genuinely embraced by dioceses and congregations around the world, which has in turn fostered a respectful and often fraternal relationship between Jewish and Christian faith leaders. But a myth powered by Gospel and soaked in two millennia of art, culture and tradition is difficult to fully dispel.

The contemporary Catholic writer E. Michael Jones declared, "Catholics have lost every single battle in the culture wars because they cannot bring themselves to say the word Jew. Because they cannot say the word Jew, they cannot identify the enemy. Am I saying that the Jews are our enemy? Yes, the Jews are the people who killed Christ. They are enemies of the entire human race."[38]

The Syrian dictator Bashar Al-Assad told Pope John Paul II on May 6, 2001, "The Jews tried to kill the principles of all religions with the same mentality in which they betrayed Jesus Christ and the same way they tried to betray and kill the Prophet Muhammad."[39]

---

37 Declaration on the Relation of the Church to Non-Christian Religions "Nostra Aetate," Proclaimed By His Holiness Pope Paul VI on October 28, 1965, https://www.vatican.va/archive/hist_councils/ii_vatican_council/documents/vat-ii_decl_19651028_nostra-aetate_en.html.

38 Anti-Defamation League factsheet, "Deicide," https://antisemitism.adl.org/deicide/.

39 *Washington Post* editorial, "Vile Words," May 8, 2001, https://www.washingtonpost.com/archive/opinions/2001/05/08/vile-words/8878c7a5-5c1b-4f1f-80e0-c59572d7e3ae/.

The Passion Play, an annual re-enactment of the betrayal and crucifixion of Christ had since the Middle Ages served to deepen the sense of Christian community and devotion by giving powerful visual effect to the Christian belief that Jesus suffered and sacrificed for the sins of mankind. It also "flared violence against Jews as Christ-killers."[40]

Upon seeing the world's most famous Passion Play, the Oberammergau Play in Bavaria, Hitler observed that "never has the menace of Jewry been so overwhelmingly portrayed as in the presentation of what happened in the time of the Romans."[41]

In light of "Nostra Aetate," many Passion Plays were either discontinued or rescripted in sensitivity to the capacity of such productions to inspire prejudice and trigger violence.

The film "The Passion of the Christ," produced by actor and filmmaker Mel Gibson and released in 2004, reversed this process of reconciliation. It took the Passion Play to its largest audience yet and reawakened much Jewish trauma derived from the Christ-killer libel.

Gibson maintained he had no antisemitic intent, was simply acting out of devotion to his own Catholic faith and had rendered a true account of the Gospels. A team of Catholic and Jewish scholars reviewed the script prior to release of the film and found to the contrary. Their report noted that Gibson had "substantially magnified the culpability of Jews

---

40 Jane Lampman, "Capturing the Passion," *Christian Science Monitor*, July 10, 2003, https://www.csmonitor.com/2003/0710/p11s01-lire.html?entryBottomStory.

41 Cohen, *Christ Killers*, 215.

at the expense of fidelity to gospel accounts,"[42] and relied on "avaricious and bloodthirsty reiterations of the same ugly tropes that have plagued Christian representations of Jews for centuries."[43]

Gibson's interpretation of the death of Christ relied in part on a mid-nineteenth-century work, "The Dolorous Passion of our Lord Jesus Christ," written by a German nun, Anne Catherine Emmerich, who had herself deviated from Gospel and reinterpreted the Passion based on claimed "ecstatic visions of Jesus and the Virgin Mary."[44]

Her work focused less on the "moral and inspirational lessons of the Passion"[45] and filled the gaps in the Gospels with her own graphic depictions of ultra-violence, gratuitous taunting of Jesus by the Jews and the presence of the devil amongst the crowd of Jews, a liberty that found its way into Gibson's work also and had the effect of "drawing an unmistakable visual connection between the Jews and Satan."[46]

Emmerich said she had visions of "the frightful cry of the Jews, *His blood be upon us, and on our children* ... which they have entailed upon themselves, and appears to me to penetrate even to the very marrow of their bones—even to the unborn infants."[47]

---

42 Mary C. Boys, "'I Didn't See Any Anti-Semitism,'" Why Many Christians Don't Have a Problem with 'The Passion of the Christ.'" *CrossCurrents* 54, no. 1 (2004): 10.

43 Ibid.

44 Cohen, *Christ Killers*, 131.

45 Ibid., 132.

46 Boys, "'I Didn't See Any Anti-Semitism' 10.

47 Cohen, *Christ Killers*, 132.

Gibson claimed his own insight into the death of Jesus: "I know how it went down."[48]

Roger Ebert, in a generally favorable review of the film, observed that at least 100 of its 126 minutes were taken up by the graphic visuals of the torture and death of Jesus, making it "the most violent film" he had ever seen.[49]

The leadership shown by the Catholic Church in renouncing the "teaching of contempt" against Jews and the Christ-killers libel has blunted the potency of the myth of deicide. Yet the spirit of the myth persists as a willingness to accept Jewish treachery, spiritual blindness, unremitting evil and vengefulness.

Placards and cartoons depicting the crucifixion with Palestinians transposed in place of Jesus frequently appear in pro-Palestinian rallies and publications. This seeks to explain Israeli conduct in terms of a Jewish propensity for evil and positions the Palestinians as innocent, godly victims.

The massacre at the Tree of Life Synagogue in Pittsburgh in 2018 further demonstrated the enduring power of the Christ-killers myth. The gunman, Robert Bowers, cited the Gospel of John in his profile on the online chat forum Gab. John had written, in reference to the Jews, "you belong to your father, the devil and you want to carry out his desires." "All Jews must die," Bowers shouted as he murdered eleven elderly Jewish worshippers.

---

48 Mel Gibson, interview with Diane Sawyer on filming "The Passion of the Christ" (ABC, 2004).

49 Roger Ebert, review of "The Passion of the Christ," February 24, 2004, https://www.rogerebert.com/reviews/the-passion-of-the-christ-2004.

Global Domination

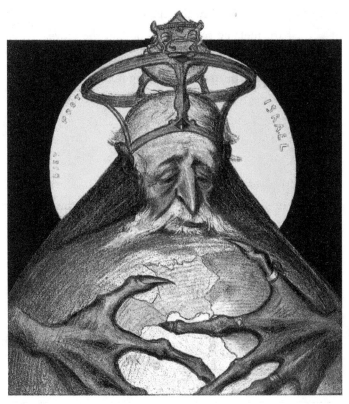

"Le roi Rothschild," cover illustration for *Le Rire*, 1898 cartoon showing
Rothschild with the world in his hands, by Charles Lucien Léandre.
Public domain, via Wikimedia Commons

The gates creaked softly; the rustling of long coats was heard, touching the stones and shrubbery; finally a vague white figure appeared and slipped by like a shadow along the pathways. This figure knelt before one of the tombstones; three times it touched the stone with its forehead and softly whispered a prayer.

At that moment the clock struck twelve. A sharp metallic sound rang out on the grave, after which a blue flame appeared and illumined the thirteen kneeling figures.

"I greet you, heads of the twelve tribes of Israel," announced a dull voice.

"We greet you, son of the accursed."

These words were first published in 1868, in the first part of a multi-volume work of fiction titled *Biarritz*, by the German novelist Hermann Otto Friedrich Goedsche (pen name Sir John Retcliffe). The chapter was titled "The Jewish Cemetery in Prague and The Council of Representatives of the Twelve Tribes of Israel."[1] It told of a secret meeting of Jewish elders, each said to represent one of the original twelve tribes of Israel and a thirteenth delegate representing the "unfortunate and exiles." The meeting took place in the ancient Jewish cemetery

---

1   Contained in Herman Bernstein, *The History of a Lie* (New York: Ogilvie Publishing Co., 1921).

of Prague at midnight, exactly one hundred years after the last such meeting.

"The future is ours!" proclaim the Jewish elders after which they proceed to elucidate, one by one, the means by which the Jews intend to "achieve power and supremacy over all other nations on earth."

"All the movable capital must go over to the hands of the Jews," announces the first elder. "If we will be supreme in the stock exchange, we will attain the same supremacy in the governments."

"The Jews should secure the possibility of acquiring real estate," declares the second. "When the land is in our hands, the labor of the Christian workers and farmers will give us a tenfold income."

Next is industry. "Transforming the artisans into our factory workers, we will be in a position to direct the masses for our political purposes."

Then the representative of the tribe of Levi speaks: "The natural enemy of the Jews is the Christian church. Therefore, we must try to humiliate it, we must instil into it free-thinking, scepticism and conflicts."

The tribe of Isaachar calls for the "downfall of the military class, to arouse suspicion in the masses against it, and to incite animosity against one another."

Zebulun "in a dull voice like a storm in the distance" urges that they "direct the movements of nation. Every kind of dissatisfaction, every revolution, increases our capital and brings us nearer to our goal."

The tribe of Dan has more modest aims. "We must get control of the traffic in liquor, butter, wool and bread."

Naftali urges the Jews to seize the arts and sciences. "A physician penetrates the secrets of families and holds their lives in his hands."

The representative of the tribe of Asher eyes the flesh of Christian women. "We enjoy the forbidden pleasure with the women of our enemies."

The tribe of Manasseh speaks. "If gold is the first power in the world, the press is the second. Our people must direct the daily publications. We are cunning, shrewd and we possess money which we know how to utilize for our purposes. With the press in our hands, we can turn wrong into right, dishonesty into honesty."

Finally, the meeting concludes. "A blue flame flares up brightly upon the grave of the Rabbi," and there appeared "a monstrous golden figure of an animal." The elders slither out of the cemetery, the last of which tells the watchman, "Close the house of life and may your lips be sealed with the seal of Solomon for a hundred years."

The witness to all this then summarizes the diabolical mission of the Jews for the benefit of the reader: "To concentrate in their hands all the capital of the nations of all lands; to secure possession of all land, railroads, mines, houses; to be at the head of all organizations, to occupy the highest governmental posts, to paralyze commerce and industry everywhere, to seize the press, to direct legislation, public opinion and national movements—and all for the purpose of subjugating all nations on earth to their power!"[2]

---

2   Contained ibid.

Goedsche's closing statement captures the essence of the myth of the Jewish global conspiracy. A lie that cast the Jew, previously branded backward, insular and inferior, as the most cunning and dangerous creature on earth.

As we will see, the myth of Jewish global domination was created and nurtured by men who while separated by nationality, status and industry, possessed remarkably similar worldviews. Each was deeply conservative in their politics and led by defective interpretations of the world around them. Each was gripped by an almost romantic nostalgia for an idealized, imagined bygone era, a world of clear social norms underpinned by Christian values. They longed for the restoration of a rigid class system led by a nobility or the fallen royal houses of Europe. Each viewed himself as a pastoralist, a Walden living a simpler, purer manner of life away from the excesses and vices of the cities. And each sought to explain a world that was rapidly changing, modernizing, industrializing, liberalizing. Lacking the clarity to do so, each attributed everything they hated or misunderstood to the Jews and lived in pursuit of their destruction.

The lie of Jewish global domination, concocted by charlatans, would provide the clearest linkage between foul words and the genocide of a people.

Goedsche's fantasy of a nocturnal cemetery tête-à-têtes chaired by a poltergeist was not the first antisemitic text warning of the Jewish peril. Martin Luther had written *On the Jews and Their Lies* in 1543 and Russian and German literature produced a steady sequence of antisemitic polemicists. But Goedsche should be credited with setting in motion a literary chain that would provide the justification for genocide.

Goedsche's book fell into the hands of Russian antisemites who published the Prague Cemetery chapter as a separate pamphlet. Then in 1881 it appeared in French, shrewdly stripped of the obviously fantastical and supernatural elements and presented as a single speech which attributed the words of each of Goedsche's thirteen Jewish elders to one Chief Rabbi said to be addressing a meeting of Jewish leaders. This spin-off work, titled *The Rabbi's Speech*, became a sensation. The *Speech* began appearing in newspapers and pamphlets across Europe. It did not matter that it was derived from a most obvious work of fiction. Nor did the fact that the British diplomat who "unearthed" this diabolical plot bore the name Sir John Retcliffe (Goedsche's own pen name) or that, as Norman Cohn traces, an 1896 French edition farcically declared the mysterious Chief Rabbi to be "Rabbi John Readclif." The document was like plutonium in the possession of anyone wishing to provoke a hatred of the Jews.

The work served another vital purpose. By identifying distinct spheres of influence which the Jews had supposedly subverted or seized, it was possible to completely discredit those institutions. The media, elected governments, professionals, academics could no longer be trusted. Perhaps most significant of all were Goedsche's words given to the representative of the tribe of Zebulun, who urged his brethren elders to "support of every kind of dissatisfaction, every revolution … as ours is a conservative nation [but] ours is a time of many reforms." In this way, every challenge to traditional authority, whether that of the crown, the autocrat, the military or the church could be sullied as Jewish manipulations to sow chaos, rather than an expression of popular will. There was no discontent, call for reform or popular uprising, only Jewish schemes. This particular feature of the myth remains in our discourse today in the form of smears that popular movements are the work of a single puppeteer, the grand strategy of a Jewish financier or media baron.

The Rabbi's Speech left the page, the self-indulgent world of treatises and refutations, and entered the real world at Kishinev in Bessarabia (today's Moldova) in 1903. On April 19, Easter Sunday, gangs of youths began roaming the streets of Kishinev smashing the windows of stores and houses owned by Jews. Emboldened by the indifference of the police and soldiers garrisoned there and receiving the blessings of the bishop who strode the streets alongside the rioters, the mob grew in size and its activities quickly escalated. A Jewish shopkeeper blind in one eye had the other eye gouged out. Some Jews had nails driven through their skulls. Women and young girls were raped.[3] The familiarity of the assailants to their victims was particularly chilling. One rape victim recalled that she had cradled her attacker in her arms when he was a baby.[4] This jarring aspect of the violence was a portent of how neighbor would turn on neighbor on a mass scale just four decades later.

The pogrom (mob attack on a Jewish community) was the first of the twentieth century and it curiously occurred in a place noted for the harmonious relations between Jews

3   Monty Noam Penkower, "The Kishinev Pogrom of 1903: A Turning Point in Jewish History," *Modern Judaism* 24, no. 3 (2004): 187–225, http://www.jstor.org/stable/1396539.

4   Polly Zavadivker, review of Steven J. Zipperstein, *Pogrom: Kishinev and the Tilt of History* (New York: Liveright, 2018), *The Journal of Modern History* 92, no. 1 (March 2020).

and non-Jews. Kishinev had refused to partake in the state-sanctioned pogroms that swept Russia through the 1880s.

The difference in 1903 was a man named Pavel Krushevan, a virulent antisemite and member of the Black Hundreds fascist movement. Krushevan had arrived in Kishinev in 1894, and after taking over the city's major newspaper began to strategically manufacture anti-Jewish hysteria. His articles accused the city's Jews of controlling the local economy and ritual murder and called for a "crusade against the hated race." Krushevan was a man of talent but deeply troubled. As the historian Steven J. Zipperstein discovered through Krushevan's personal papers, he was raised by a Jewish stepmother in great poverty, a condition Krushevan resented. He recorded in his diary that he wished he had been "born a lady," and was in love with a Cossack.[5] His torment and repressions found expression in social conservatism, authoritarian politics and a fanatical antisemitism.

Krushevan wrote of a beautiful, simple world swept away by modernity, represented by the Jew. He wrote of the splendor of the province of Bessarabia, its meadows, rivers and woods. With equal flair, he recruited his countrymen to antisemitism, conveying a message that "the Jewish march toward world hegemony clashed with Russia's existence and must be

---

5   Jack Miles, "Inventing the Pogrom: Assigning Meaning to the Kishinev Massacre," review of Steven J. Zipperstein, *Pogrom: Kishinev and the Tilt of History* (New York: Liveright, 2018), *LA Review of Books*, April 9, 2018, https://lareviewofbooks.org/article/inventing-the-pogrom-assigning-meaning-to-the-kishinev-massacre.

stopped."[6] It yielded the desired result. The attack on the Jews of Kishinev began in the plunder of liquor and tobacco stores, then the destruction of property and burning of homes, then gang rape, murder, sadism. Two thousand left homeless, some five hundred dead or wounded, two babies among the dead, all in the name of throttling the Jewish plot to enslave the world, which was apparently playing out in the town of Kishinev.

The chief of police said, "it serves the Jews right."[7] A visiting foreign journalist noted that in the immediate aftermath of the devastation there was "neither regret nor remorse."[8] In the period leading up to the pogrom, Krushevan had distributed copies of *The Rabbi's Speech* throughout the city.

The dark power of the global domination myth and of Krushevan only grew after Kishinev. Krushevan is an arch-villain who should enjoy greater infamy. Zipperstein pegged him as "one of the vilest fabulists of modern times."[9] He plotted, subverted, misled, peddled disinformation by seizing the media, duped the masses, and all for an exceedingly violent and destructive purpose.

Krushevan saw the international outrage to the pogrom as further evidence that the Jews controlled government and the media. Why else would papers and politicians express

6   "Pogrom: Kishinev and the Tilt of History," Public Seminar, July 2018, https://publicseminar.org/2018/07/pogrom-kishinev-and-the-tilt-of-history/.

7   Monty Noam Penkower, "The Kishinev Pogrom of 1903: A Turning Point in Jewish History," *Modern Judaism* 24, no. 3 (2004): 189 note 6.

8   Ibid., 188.

9   Corydon Ireland, "The Pogrom that Transformed 20th Century Jewry," *The Harvard Gazette*, April 9, 2009, https://news.harvard.edu/gazette/story/2009/04/the-pogrom-that-transformed-20th-century-jewry/.

sympathy for people who had merely gotten what they deserved?

Krushevan was then sent to St. Petersburg to run a newspaper called *Znamya*. Now with his audience no longer a remote province but the imperial capital, just a few months later, Krushevan performed his greatest feat.

From August 26 to September 7, 1903, Krushevan's newspaper published a document that very much borrowed on the themes of Goedsche's scene in the Prague Cemetery and its derivative, *The Rabbi's Speech*. But while the earlier works receded into obscurity, the new document would become the most notorious forgery ever produced, what the historian Norman Cohn called the "warrant for genocide," *The Protocols of the Elders of Zion*.

The introduction to the edition of *The Protocols* translated from the Russian by Victor E. Marsden, the Russia correspondent for the *Morning Post* newspaper, explains that *Protocols* refer to the minutes of proceedings of a secret meeting of the "innermost rulers of Zion." Marsden declares in the introduction that denials of the authenticity of *The Protocols* are "in itself an admission of their genuineness." As to the identity of these Elders? Marsden says, "this is a secret which has not been revealed."[10]

As much as Goedsche's work of fantasy was at least imaginative, memorable and arguably competently written, *The Protocols* make for unbearable reading, rambling,

---

10 *Protocols of the Learned Elders of Zion*, trans. Victor Marsden (Reedy, WV: Liberty Bell Publications, 1970), 5, https://archive.org/details/ protocolsofthelearnedeldersofzion_201905/page/n5/mode/2up.

disjointed and in parts, inscrutable. Unlike Goedsche's work, *The Protocols* were likely constructed not by a single author but by an assortment of figures, of which Krushevan himself may have been one.

Much of the text of *The Protocols* was also lifted from another work, *Dialogue aux Enfers entre Montesquieu et Machiavel*, by Maurice Joly, a satirical work mocking the despotism of Napoleon III, and bearing no connection to the Jews whatsoever. Joly's work was virtually unknown and suppressed in France because of its subversiveness and this made it ripe for plagiarism.

The Protocols consist of twenty-four points, setting out how the Jews intend to take over the world, through the now familiar themes of plundering the world's gold, controlling the press and bringing chaos through the spread of liberalism.

The publishers of *The Protocols*, from Krushevan onwards, offered completely different explanations for who was supposed to have issued the files, how they were obtained and why they are in parts identical to Joly's work. It hardly mattered. Those who chose to believe this "atrociously written reactionary balderdash,"[11] simply shrugged at every exposé of its fraudulence and went on believing it because they liked what it said.

After Krushevan ran *The Protocols* in St. Petersburg, they appeared in church sermons, pamphlets, newspapers and then in a book by Sergei Nilus, a kook who drifted into the occult and religious dogma after suffering financial ruin and who

11   Norman Cohn, *Warrant for Genocide* (London: Serif, 2005), 81.

is sometimes credited with being the original author of *The Protocols*.

The fall of Europe's last absolute monarchy, in Russia in 1917, raised *The Protocols* to the level of prophecy. Owing to the Tsar's catalogue of antisemitic laws, the Jews had hitherto been invisible in public life in Russia. The Bolshevik leadership was comprised of many previously oppressed minorities. Indeed, that oppression stimulated the involvement of Caucasians, Armenians, Poles, Latvians and Jews in disproportionately high numbers. But to the sinister or weak of mind, the presence of Jews in the leadership confirmed that the Revolution was not the culmination of the cruelty and degradation heaped on the people by four hundred years of feudalism, but the embodiment of the Jewish global domination plot. In a country wracked by political upheaval and popular discontent, *The Protocols* seemed to answer every question.

As the 1917 Revolution gave way to civil war in Russia, the members of the ultra-nationalist Black Hundreds became embedded with the White Army which sought to restore the monarchy and vanquish Bolshevism. Copies of *The Protocols* were now being printed across Russia and distributed to frontline troops.

Between 1917 and 1921, some two thousand pogroms on Jewish communities were carried out resulting in the deaths of as many as two hundred thousand Jewish civilians. In Fastov, near Kyiv, Jews were simply shot on sight. One soldier said, "we had leave to have a party for three days."[12]

---

12   Ibid., 136.

Women in their seventies were gang-raped in front of husbands and daughters. Sons were made to hang their own fathers. Victims were burned or buried alive, hanged to the point of near asphyxiation then taken down and subjected to some other form of torture. It is not possible to comprehend what depravity drove men to carry out such acts. Nor is it possible to discern the precise extent to which *The Protocols* and the Jewish global domination myth motivated these outrages. Granted, historically it had taken little literary inspiration to unleash frenzied Cossack attacks on Jewish villages. Bogdan Chemlnitski's horsemen slaughtered some one hundred thousand and the later scenes of bloodlust and vulgarity were precisely as described in accounts of Chemnlitski's campaign in the seventeenth century. State sanctioned pogroms had occurred in the 1880s.

But the White Army's pogroms were used as a tactic of war directed by the officer corps, among whom the belief in a Jewish menace was rampant and the terms "Jew" and "Bolshevik" had become interchangeable. A British war correspondent travelling with the army of Anton Denikin, reported that "the officers and men of the Army laid practically all blame for their country's troubles on the Hebrew. They held that the whole cataclysm had been engineered by some great and mysterious society of international Jews, who, in the pay and at the orders of Germany, had seized the psychological moment and taken the reins of government."[13]

---

13 John Ernest Hodgson, *With Denikin's Armies: Being a Description of the Cossak Counter-Revolution in South Russia, 1918–1920* (London: Temple Bar Publishing Co., 1932), 54–56.

Following the consolidation of power by the Bolsheviks, many Black Hundreds, reactionaries and Tsarist loyalists fled to western Europe bringing stories of Judeo-Bolshevik barbarism and copies of *The Protocols* with them. Had *The Protocols* arrived in Germany at another time, the work would likely have been catalogued among other antisemitic texts and mattered little. But their entry coincided with the defeat of Germany in World War I, the Treaty of Versailles and a crippling, humiliating settlement imposed on Germany. To add to the climate of suspicion and betrayal, the theories of Ernst Haeckel and Hans Gunther on social Darwinism, racial hierarchies and the notion that ethnic groups possess distinct, immutable tendencies and intellectual and moral qualities, were beginning to take hold. This now meant that the conduct attributed to the Jews could not be cured through the baptismal waters, ensuring that the only measures deemed capable of stopping the Jewish plot had to be complete and final.

Unsurprisingly, the rise of Nazism saw *The Protocols* take on a nearly scriptural dimension. Hitler saw a global Jewish conspiracy in everything, and *The Protocols* were an excellent means of turning ordinary middle-class Germans into anti-semites, making them complicit or at least indifferent to what would be done to the Jews.

Norman Cohn relates an account of a public lecture on *The Protocols* in 1920s Germany: "In Berlin I attended several meetings which were devoted entirely to *The Protocols*. I observed the students. A few hours earlier they had perhaps been exerting all their mental energy in a seminar under guidance of a world-famous scholar. Now young blood was boiling, eye flashed, fists clenched, hoarse voices roared applause or vengeance."[14] Seeing its impact on young minds, the Nazis made *The Protocols* a prescribed text for study in German schools.[15]

Hitler had referred to *The Protocols* in his manifesto, *Mein Kampf*. "For when once this book becomes generally familiar to a people," he said, "the Jewish menace can be regarded as already vanquished."[16]

Through *The Rabbi's Speech* and *The Protocols*, Krushevan had taken the myth of a Jewish conspiracy to achieve global domination from the realm of petty bigotry and paranoia to the courts of tsars and the classrooms of millions. Hitler would take the matter to its natural conclusion, executing the warrant to annihilate the race that lurked behind every misfortune. Between these two men sits another, one seized by the same mania, whose restless fanaticism compelled him to do whatever was necessary for the world to share in his hatred. That man was Henry Ford.

During a camping trip in 1919, a friend recalled Ford lecturing the others around the campfire "attributing all evil to the Jews or to the Jewish capitalists. The Jews caused the war, the Jews caused the outbreak of thieving and robbery all over the country, the Jews caused the inefficiency of the navy."[17]

What made Ford so dangerous was that he was not a literary man, content to release his prejudices onto the page. He

---

14   Cohn, *Warrant for Genocide*, 151.

15   Ibid., 45.

16   Adolf Hitler, *Mein Kampf*, 11th ed. (Munich, 1942), 337.

17   "Ford's Antisemitism," PBS, https://www.pbs.org/wgbh/american experience/features/henryford-antisemitism/.

was a builder, a doer and a salesman and when motivated to bring a concept into existence he knew only to do it with maximum impact. He acquired the unknown local paper *Dearborn Independent* in 1919, and proceeded to raid the editorial team of the *Detroit News* to lure top hatchet men and tabloid reporters. Never content with mediocrity, Ford ensured the paper was distributed not only in Dearborn but through every Ford dealership in the country. Often copies were tossed into newly sold Model T Fords. By 1927, Ford had sold 15 million Model Ts and Ford's small-town paper was one of the highest circulating in the country.

Beginning in May 1920, ninety-one consecutive weekly editions of the paper contained attacks on the Jews, beginning with the front-page article of May 22, 1920 devoted to the global Jewish conspiracy, titled "The International Jew: The World's Problem." The front-page article alone accused the Jews of controlling the media, business and real estate. The paper blamed the Jews for the advent of jazz music, so-called "moron music."[18]

In the classic style of the conspiracy theorist, every implausibility and paradox were waved away as an added piece of intrigue. "The Jew is the world's enigma. Poor in his masses, he yet controls the world's finances."[19]

---

18 Ronnie Schreiber, "How Henry Ford, Who Published Racist Diatribes Against Jazz, Helped Popularize the Sound of Jazz and R&B," February 4, 2020, https://www.thetruthaboutcars.com/2020/01/how-henry-ford-who-published-racist-diatribes-against-jazz-helped-popularize-the-sound-of-jazz-and-rb/.

19 Bill McGraw, "Henry Ford and the Jews, the Story Dearborn Didn't Want Told," February 4, 2019, https://www.bridgemi.com/

The worst of the articles were then bound up in a four-edition work published between 1920 and 1922, titled *The International Jew*. Deliberately left un-copyrighted to enable its free distribution, the book reached the world through Ford's unparalleled wealth and means of distribution. It reached Germany in 1922 and is credited with helping Hitler formulate his world view of "conspiratorial antisemitism." Hitler claimed Ford to be "his inspiration" and kept a portrait of the industrialist in his Munich office.[20]

In his war crimes trial at Nuremberg, the head of the Hitler Youth, Baldur von Shirach, testified that "the decisive antisemitic book which influenced my colleagues was Henry Ford's book, *The International Jew*; I read it and became antisemitic. In those days this book made such a deep impression on my friends and myself because we saw in Henry Ford the representative of success, also the exponent of a progressive social policy. In the poverty-stricken and wretched Germany of the time, youth looked toward America, and it was Henry Ford who to us represented America."[21]

The global domination myth served a distinct function in the spread of violent antisemitism. The notion of the scheming, diabolical Jew had already entered the psyche through the charges of blood libel and deicide. But these pitted the Jew against the Christian and attributed the malice and jealousy

---

michigan-government/henry-ford-and-jews-story-dearborn-didnt-want-told.

20   Ibid.

21   Nuremberg Trial Proceedings, vol. 14, 147th day, Thursday, May 23, 1946, Morning Session, Avalon Project, Yale Law School, https://avalon.law.yale.edu/imt/05-23-46.asp.

of the Jews to their spiritual blindness and refusal to adopt the faiths of the majority. Accepting Christ could still cure all that. The global domination myth was rooted in the same characterization of the Jews, but went much further.

It insisted they were not content with taking revenge on a Christian child here and there on the Passover, but they schemed to destroy the world. This gave antisemitism an extraordinary potency and a unifying quality that far exceeded that of religious antisemitism. By enlarging the menace from a backward, superstitious presence in the synagogue and the ghetto to a great serpent that straddles the globe, it also necessitated more comprehensive forms of self-defense and punishment. If the sentence for ritual murder was forcible conversion or public burning, what would be a fitting response to enslaving all humanity?

The emergence of Bolshevism from one of many revolutionary factions in Russia into the absolute power of the Soviet Union, proved that the global Jewish conspiracy was rampant. War with the international Jew or Judeo-Bolshevism could not be deferred any longer. Hitler told the Reichstag in January 1939 that it was the international Jew leading the world to war, and he was explicit in what he intended to do to it: "If the international Finance-Jewry inside and outside of Europe should succeed in plunging the peoples of the earth once again into a world war, the result will be not the Bolshevization of earth, and thus a Jewish victory, but the annihilation of the Jewish race in Europe."[22]

---

22 Adolf Hitler, speech to Reichstag, January 30, 1939, https://www.ushmm.org/learn/timeline-of-events/1939-1941/hitler-speech-to-german-parliament.

It followed that the Nazi invasion of the Soviet Union on June 22, 1941, a strike against the center of Judeo-Bolshevism, was conducted like no other war. Hitler termed it *Rassenkampf* or race war, implemented a starvation plan to depopulate the country and deployed elite killing squads known as Einsatzgruppen to commence the complete annihilation of the Jews, a policy that gained formal assent at Wannsee in January 1942, where the "final solution to the Jewish question" became official policy. This completed the process started with lurid texts and printed pamphlets.

The myth of global Jewish domination justified, indeed necessitated, everything that was done to the Jews under cover of war, an industrial crime but one ultimately carried out by hundreds of thousands of individuals operating at close quarters. The German soldier who shot Jews in forest pits, the Balt who pushed Jews into gas chambers, the Hungarian who shot Jewish children into the Danube, each had to justify their act, reconcile it with their moral code, as much as the henchmen at Wannsee had done. Ridding the world of its greatest menace, protecting one's homeland and family from the ruin the Jew planned to heap on them, were sound reasons indeed, sufficient to placate the conscience long enough to dispatch six million Jewish men, women and children.

Today, *The Protocols* and *The International Jew* are widely available around the world through Amazon, Apple, Barnes & Noble and other mainstream booksellers. In 2002, a blockbuster multi-part series from Egypt which incorporated *The Protocols* aired to an audience in the tens of millions. The show's co-writer and lead actor told Al-Jazeera that regardless of whether or not *The Protocols* were authentic,

"Zionism exists and it has controlled the world since the dawn of history."[23]

In a CNN segment which aired on May 22, 2021 covering the escalation between Israel and Hamas, the Pakistani Foreign Minister spoke of "deep pockets" of "very influential people" who "control the media." In a logical contortion of the Krushevan variety, a spokesperson for the Ministry later remarked that the criticism of the Foreign Minister's remarks "proved the very point he was making."[24]

The white nationalists marching in Charlottesville, Virginia during the Unite the Right rally in August 2017 chanted "Jews will not replace us,"[25] invoking the conspiracy theory that powerful Jewish interests are plotting to overthrow white society by strategically instigating the mass migration of non-Europeans to the United States. Robert Bowers, the Pittsburgh Synagogue gunman, adhered to the same idea.

In 2017, a former CIA operative tweeted an article titled "America's Jews are driving America's wars."[26] In 2004, the

---

23 Daniel J. Wakin, "Anti-Semitic 'Elders of Zion' Gets New Life on Egypt TV," *New York Times*, October 26, 2002, https://www.nytimes.com/2002/10/26/world/anti-semitic-elders-of-zion-gets-new-life-on-egypt-tv.html.

24 Bianna Golodryga and Emmet Lyons, "Pakistan's Top Diplomat Makes Anti-Semitic Remark during CNN Interview about Gaza Conflict," CNN, May 22, 2021, https://edition.cnn.com/2021/05/21/world/pakistan-diplomat-gaza-interview-intl/index.html.

25 Sarah Wildman, "'You will not replace us': A French Philosopher Explains the Charlottesville Chant," Vox, August 15, 2017, https://www.vox.com/world/2017/8/15/16141456/renaud-camus-the-great-replacement-you-will-not-replace-us-charlottesville-white.

26 Sophie Tatum, "Ex-CIA Operative Apologizes for Tweet of Anti-Semitic Article," CNN, September 21, 2017 https://edition.cnn.com/2017/09/21/politics/valerie-plame-wilson-tweet/index.html.

Canadian magazine *Adbusters*, which first called for the mass protests resulting in the Occupy Wall Street movement, ran an article titled "Why Won't Anyone Say They're Jewish," which contained a photo gallery of supposed framers of US foreign policy with black marks identifying the ones believed to be of Jewish ancestry.[27]

In response to an outcry over the piece, Editor Kalle Lasn maintained his position, defending it with the classic tones of global Jewish domination, "they are no ordinary group—they are the most influential political/intellectual force in the world right now. They have the power to start wars and to stop them. They are the prime architects of America's foreign policy since 9/11."[28] Lasn was referring to the political movement of neo-conservatism, but to Lasn, the neo-cons were virtually all Jews, just as to the White Army, the Bolsheviks were all Jews. Kanye West then elevated the practice of identifying, counting and outing Jews in positions of prominence in the belief that any multiple of Jews must be engaged in a conspiracy or controlling behavior to advance their sinful interests at the expense of decent folk. In reality of course, most Jews do not know each other and those who do are likely to be separated by political, personal, ethical and other considerations, as are all people. If Jews are represented in certain

---

27 David Brooks, "The Milquetoast Radicals," *New York Times*, October 10, 2011, https://www.nytimes.com/2011/10/11/opinion/the-milquetoast-radicals.html?_r=2&partner=rssnyt&emc=rss%20 http://mediamatters.org/mmtv/201110110012.

28 Drew Grant, "Much Ado About 'Adbusters' Relationship to the Jews," *Observer*, October 20, 2011, https://observer.com/2011/10/much-ado-about-adbusters-relationship-to-the-jews/.

industries at greater rates than their percentage of the overall population, there may be, cultural or historical factors that drew them to certain vocations over others, as occurs with many ethnic groups. The antisemite is quick to identify Jews in unpopular industries, formerly moneylending, now media, finance and entertainment, but rarely credits Jews for being overrepresented in medical research, technology, innovation or philanthropic giving to cancer research and palliative care. The antisemite also ignores the other characteristics common to individuals in senior positions, which might include membership in a golf club, ownership of a German car or an Ivy League education. Instead, the individuals are stripped of all human qualities other than Jewish ancestry, because this alone is sufficient to demonstrate evil intentions or evil deeds.

But it is difficult to rationally explain or refute something motivated by a defect in reasoning. The fact that *The Protocols* were definitively proven to be a piece of fraud based on plagiarism in several legal proceedings and numerous dispassionate scholarly investigations, never undermined its appeal. Ford said that regardless of whether they were authentic, "they fit in with what is going on."[29]

And so survives this most terrible piece of mythology. Seductive by virtue of providing a neat, clear explanation for all human misfortune, it now moves from social media into cities just as the same ravings leapt from the pages of *The Rabbi's Speech* into the homes of the Jews of Kishinev.

---

29 *Protocols of the Learned Elders of Zion*, edition retained in FBI archives along with accompanying correspondence, https://vault.fbi.gov/protocols-of-learned-elders-of-zion/protocols-of-learned-elders-of-zion-part-01-of-01.

MYTH 4

Chosen

Le Roi de France... le voilà!

"Le Roi de France… le voila!," Marien Morazzani.
Public domain, via Wikimedia Commons

> "Do they still consider themselves the Chosen People?"
>
> —Sister Teresa Magiera, Mother Superior,
>
> Carmelite Convent, Auschwitz

A standard question used in polling to detect antisemitic attitudes is whether the respondent agrees that "Jews think they're better than other people."[1] The belief that the Jews as a people think they're superior to others and hold others in contempt runs through the vast history of antisemitism. While it is more subtle than accusations of deicide or blood libel, it serves as a highly effective adjunct that reinforces and validates other myths. This supposed superiority complex is advanced to explain why Jews would collude and scheme, harbor a loathing for Christians and disregard innocent non-Jewish life. The Malaysian prime minister Mahathir Mohamad claimed, "the Jews rule the world by proxy. They must never think they are the Chosen People."[2]

On a more emotional level, to be perceived as arrogant, as viewing oneself as intellectually and morally superior to others, is a repellent quality that arouses immediate animosity, even a desire to see that person humiliated. The persecution of the Jews throughout history was committed not with the solemnity of a state execution of a condemned prisoner, but with relish, a feeling of poetic justice that this arrogant nation was being taught a lesson and brought low.

---

1   Ben Quinn, "Almost Half of Britons Hold Antisemitic View, Poll Suggests," January 14, 2015, *Guardian*, https://www.theguardian.com/world/2015/jan/14/uk-jewish-antisemitism-rise-yougov-poll.

2   "Mahathir Fires Parting Shots," October 31, 2003, CNN, http://edition.cnn.com/2003/WORLD/asiapcf/southeast/10/30/mahathir.retire/index.html.

But where does this belief in Jewish arrogance come from? It is derived from the biblical concept that the Jews are God's "Chosen People." As we will see, being "chosen" according to the biblical tradition is a complex theological idea that carries with it covenants, reciprocal obligations, and the heavy burden to live righteously or face destruction.

Taken in its most reductionist, literal form, it can be interpreted as a form of exceptionalism, something to be found in the traditions of the other Abrahamic religions and many modern nations and historic empires. But for no other faith or nation does it attract such scorn.

Indeed, Sigmund Freud suggested the chosen concept was the very origin of antisemitism. "The deeper motives of antisemitism have their roots in time long past ... I venture to assert that the jealousy that the Jews evoked in other people by maintaining that they were the first-born, the favourite child of God the Father, has not yet been overcome by others."[3]

The idea that the Jews are God's "Chosen People" is derived from the Hebrew Bible and is affirmed in both the New Testament and in the Koran. Precisely what it means to be "chosen," by whom, and for what purpose has been the subject of theological debate for centuries.

The book of Deuteronomy contains the passage, "For you are a people holy to the Lord your God. The Lord your God has chosen you out of all the peoples on the face of the earth to be his people, his treasured possession."[4]

---

3   Avi Beker, *The Chosen: The History of an Idea, the Anatomy of an Obsession* (London: Palgrave Macmillan, 2008), 2.

4   Book of Deuteronomy 7:6.

In the original covenant between God and Abraham, God promises to Abraham that "I will give you many, many descendants," "you will be the ancestor of many nations," and "I will give you and your descendants the land in which you are immigrants, the whole land of Canaan, as an enduring possession. And I will be their God."[5] As a "symbol of the covenant between us,"[6] God commands Abraham and the Jewish people in perpetuity to perform the act of male circumcision on the eighth day after birth.

As Rabbi Gilbert S. Rosenthal notes, this concept of "choseness" was not a special status conferred on a people who possessed something inherently superior. Rather, it was a call to fulfil a purpose.

That mission, that purpose, was to serve as the first monotheistic faith, be a "light unto the nations" by demonstrating that the belief in a single, benevolent god in place of the worship of idols, would usher in a system of ethical living. These ethics would hold human life to be sacred and implored a way of living that was not impulsive and anarchic but focused on one's place within wider society and the arc of humanity. Yehezkel Kaufmann notes that the ultimate purpose of this was to "curb human arrogance, end violence, lust, greed, extreme chauvinism and warfare, and usher in a new society."[7]

As described in the book of Isaiah, this would create a utopia where the nations "shall beat their swords into ploughshares,

---

5   Book of Genesis 17:2–8.

6   Ibid. 17:11.

7   Yehezkel Kaufmann, *Toledot Ha-Emunah Ha-Yisraelit* (Jerusalem: Mosad Bialik, 1953), vol. 3, bk. 1, 255f.

and their spears into pruning hooks," a world where "nation shall not lift up sword against nation, neither shall they learn war anymore."[8]

The philosopher Martin Buber described this mission as being to "lead the way to righteousness and justice."[9]

The means by which the Jews would seek to fulfill their mission, as they saw it, was through observance of the Torah and the 613 commandments (*mitzvot*) regulating conduct and establishing morality such as avoiding slander,[10] loving one's neighbor as yourself,[11] and recognizing man's inherent fallibility, prohibiting conduct that could lead one to abandon one's traditions and eventually abandon the moral code that went with it. The use of fortune tellers was therefore prohibited[12] as was tattooing one's skin.[13]

Leviticus 26 sets out with a haunting specificity the reward for fulfilling this mission and the horrors that awaited if the Jewish people strayed from it:

> If you follow my decrees and are careful to obey my commands, I will send you rain in its season, and the ground will yield its crops and the trees their fruit and you will eat all the food you want and live in safety in your land.

---

8   Book of Isaiah 2:4.
9   Martin Buber, *Israel and the World* (New York: Schocken, 1948), 185–187.
10   Book of Leviticus 19:16.
11   Ibid. 19:18.
12   Ibid. 19:31.
13   Ibid. 19:28.

I will grant peace in the land, and you will lie down and no one will make you afraid. Your enemies will fall by the sword before you. I will look on you with favor and make you fruitful and increase your numbers, and I will keep my covenant with you.[14]

But if you will not listen to me and carry out all these commands, and if you reject my decrees and abhor my laws and fail to carry out all my commands and so violate my covenant, then I will do this to you: I will bring on you sudden terror, wasting diseases and fever that will destroy your sight and sap your strength. You will plant seed in vain, because your enemies will eat it. I will set my face against you so that you will be defeated by your enemies; those who hate you will rule over you, and you will flee even when no one is pursuing you.

If in spite of this you still do not listen to me but continue to be hostile toward me, then in my anger I will be hostile toward you, and I myself will punish you for your sins seven times over. You will eat the flesh of your sons and the flesh of your daughters. As for those of you who are left, I will make their hearts so fearful in the lands of their enemies that the sound of a windblown leaf will put them to flight. They will run as though fleeing from

---

14   Ibid. 26:3–9.

the sword, and they will fall, even though no one is pursuing them. They will stumble over one another as though fleeing from the sword, even though no one is pursuing them. So you will not be able to stand before your enemies. You will perish among the nations; the land of your enemies will devour you.[15]

The concept of being chosen is not a belief in receiving God's unqualified favor or being endowed with superior qualities. It is a duty to live a life of devotion and sacrifice that will bring a joyous life on earth or else ruin beyond all imagination.

Abraham Joshua Heschel said that "the idea of a chosen people does not suggest the preference for a people based upon a discrimination among a number of peoples. We do not say that we are superior people." Rabbi Abba Hillel Silver described the concept of being chosen not as "an accolade of self-glorification but a hard discipline of self-purification."[16]

If one were to ignore the biblical sources and the unambiguous rabbinical interpretations of what it actually means to be the chosen people, and assume the concept is in fact an expression that the Jewish faith is superior to all other belief systems, one might ask, so what?

American history and national identity are animated by concepts of "exceptionalism" such as manifest destiny. John Winthrop's reference to America as "a city upon a hill—the

15 Ibid. 26:14–38.
16 Beker, *The Chosen*, 35.

eyes of all people are upon us,"[17] is a phrase cited by presidents and presidential candidates to denote a country that is to serve as a beacon to the world, a "God-blessed"[18] country as Ronald Reagan called it, a land "watched by all the world," according to Barack Obama. Christianity holds that salvation is only found through a belief in the divinity of Jesus.[19] The "Nostra Aetate" document boldly affirms that "the Church is the new people of God."[20] The Quran states that "Islam is the religion in the sight of Allah."[21] China has been known to its people as the Central Kingdom, a term denoting "self-confidence" and the nation's claimed role as "the centre of civilisation or even the world."[22]

What's more, in each of these cases, that belief in a unique destiny and exclusivity has been boldly declared and projected outward, leading to expansionism, conquest and attempts to impose their systems on others, often by force. Judaism on the other hand is a non-proselytizing faith.

And yet, only the Jewish claim to a divine mission arouses such revulsion and scorn. Avi Beker argues the deliberate distortion of the chosen concept "lies behind the myths about

---

17 President Ronald Reagan, Farewell Address to the Nation, January 11, 1989, https://www.reaganlibrary.gov/011189i.

18 President Barack Obama, University of Massachusetts at Boston Commencement Address, June 2, 2006, http://obamaspeeches. com/074-University-of-Massachusetts-at-Boston-Commencement-Address-Obama-Speech.htm.

19 Epistle to the Romans 10:9.

20 "Nostra Aetate."

21 Quran 3:19.

22 Dr Stan Florek, "Middle Kingdom," Australian Museum, September 3, 2020, https://australian.museum/learn/cultures/international-collection/chinese/middle-kingdom/.

Jewish conspiracies and perceived Jewish power and is the prime source of hatred towards Jews."[23]

Today, the myth of Jewish arrogance derived from being chosen is a mainstay of antisemitic discourse and online chatter. It presents as a snide reference to Jews believing they're better than others or as an explanation for supposed Jewish impunity or callousness.

These feelings of contempt, diagnosed as jealousy by Freud, have spawned entire movements intent on "replacing" the Jews as God's chosen people and "proving" this replacement by maintaining the Jews in a condition of inferiority.

Arnold Toynbee observed that the Jews "involuntarily begot two Judaic world religions (Christianity and Islam) whose millions (now billions) of adherents make the preposterous but redoubtable claim to have superseded the Jews, by the Jewish God."[24]

Rabbi Moritz Gudeman of Vienna identifies the great puzzle confronting the monotheistic faiths that followed Judaism. "The Christian kneels before the image of a Jew, wrings his hands before the image of a Jewess, his Apostles, Festivals, and Psalms are Jewish," he wrote.[25]

The Jews are the central player in the shared Abrahamic tradition, the originators of the radical belief in a single god that swept the world, and a people plainly stated to have been chosen to enter into a covenant with the Almighty. Yet in order for Christianity and Islam and their new texts to have any validity,

---

23   Beker, *The Chosen*, 3.
24   Ibid., 39.
25   Ibid.

the Jews had to be rejected. Otherwise, if they were accepted as the custodians of this ancient covenant and a people with a mission from God, how could offshoot faiths that depart from the Hebrew bible claim to be the true faith and the recipients of God's favor? This problem is solved by recasting the Jew as a corruption of himself, a people gone astray that are unrecognizable from the Jews of Moses, the prophets, and kings. Yes, the Jews were chosen, but they have since been "unchosen," and replaced by worthier peoples.

As Avi Beker observes, Christianity had to "maintain the Jews in their inferior position so as to prove the transfer of election from the Jew to the Christian."[26] The dhimmi status conferred on Jews in Islamic lands served a similar purpose. It maintained the Jew in a permanent position of inferiority, so that the comparatively privileged status of the Muslim could attest to the favor of the Lord passing from Jew to Muslim.

"There cannot be two Chosen People. We are God's people,"[27] Hitler declared in the clearest expression of this replacement theology.

Faith leaders have for the most part played a constructive role in rejecting replacement theology and avoiding the sort of crude, reductionist interpretations of the chosen concept that give rise to the myth of Jewish arrogance. The historic declaration on the relations of the Church to non-Christian religions, "Nostra Aetate," expressly rejected replacement theology: "The Church, therefore, cannot forget that she received

26 Ibid., 48.
27 Hermann Rauschning, *Hitler Speaks—A Series of Political Conversations on His Real Aims* (London: Thornton Butterworth, 1940), 234, 238.

the revelation of the Old Testament through the people with whom God in His inexpressible mercy concluded the Ancient Covenant."[28] As Pope John Paul II stated, that covenant "was never revoked."[29]

Yet the wilful distortion of the chosen concept is still used to incite hatred by those inclined to do so. Louis Farrakhan, the leader of the Nation of Islam movement in the United States, frequently preaches on this theme:

> "The Chosen of God" and that Israel, or Palestine, belongs to you; I want to disabuse you of that … And I'm going to tell you about your future: You that think you have power to frighten and dominate the peoples of the world. I am here to announce the end of your time.[30]
>
> How could they be the chosen of God and leading the world into filth and indecency?[31]

---

28   "Nostra Aetate."

29   Pope John Paul II, Address to Representatives of the West German Jewish Community Mainz, West Germany, November 17, 1980, https://www.catholicsforisrael.com/articles/jewish-christian-relations/235-john-paul-ii-address-to-reps-of-west-german-jewish-community.

30   Louis Farrakhan, Saviours' Day speech (part 1), February, 19, 2017, https://www.adl.org/education/resources/reports/nation-of-islam-farrakhan-in-his-own-words.

31   Louis Farrakhan, speech at Mosque Maryam, Chicago, IL, March 10, 2010, https://www.adl.org/education/resources/reports/nation-of-islam-farrakhan-in-his-own-words.

The founder of Israel's Islamic Movement, Sheikh Abdallah Nimr Darwish, declared, "We are the chosen people of the world. In the long run we will all meet at one point and make Jerusalem the capital of a Palestinian state."[32]

Replacement theology has not only pitted Jews against non-Jews in a contrived battle for God's favor, but it has also spawned rather peculiar formulations to reconcile the chosen status conferred in the Old Testament with a perception of Jewish inferiority and unworthiness.

In the calculus of the Black Hebrew Israelite Movement, a vehemently supremacist sect that preaches hatred from American street-corners, the covenant between God and the Jewish people is real and has not been replaced, but the "authentic" Israel with whom the covenant was made are not Jews but Black Hebrew Israelites. They fanatically maintain that the Jews of today are "imposters."[33] In December 2019, a follower of the Black Hebrew Israelite Movement, Grafton E. Thomas, entered the home of a rabbi in Monsey, New York during a Channukah celebration and murdered one man with a machete, wounding four others.[34] The shooting of six people

32 Francis X. Clines, "4 Palestinians Die in Day of Protest Against Israel," New York Times, March 31, 1988, https://www.nytimes.com/1988/03/31/world/4-palestinians-die-in-day-of-protest-against-israel.html.

33 Daniel Burke, "Who Are the Black Hebrew Israelites?," CNN, December 12, 2019, https://edition.cnn.com/2019/12/11/us/hebrew-black-israelites-jersey-city/index.html.

34 Rebecca Liebson, Christina Goldbaum, Joseph Goldstein and Nicholas Bogel-Burroughs, "Intruder Screamed 'I'll Get You' in Attack on Jews at Rabbi's Home," New York Times, December 29, 2019, https://www.nytimes.com/2019/12/29/nyregion/monsey-new-york-stabbing.html.

at a kosher supermarket in Jersey City, also in December 2019, was perpetrated by another apparent follower of the Black Hebrew Israelite Movement.[35]

Rabbi Lord Immanuel Jakobovits suggested that all peoples are chosen for their own unique purpose and contribution to humanity. For the Jews, this means "pioneering religion and morality."[36] To a great extent, the explanations of those like Rabbi Jakobovits, for whom the chosen concept confers awe and humility rather than arrogance, do not matter. Those who hold the Jews in contempt continue to deploy the chosen concept as a sneering punchline, the blatant proof of Jewish chauvinism and a justification for everything meted out to them.

George Bernard Shaw exemplified this mindset when he called the chosen concept "a monstrous presumption" which constitutes "a dangerous paranoiac delusion." The Jews "who still want to be the chosen race should go to Palestine and stew in their own juice," he said. "The rest had better stop being Jews and start being human beings."[37]

These reactions to the chosen concept are indicative of the cruel and often perplexing treatment reserved for Jews throughout history. The Jew is edited out of their own story,

35 Michael Gold and Ali Watkins, "Suspect in Jersey City Linked to Black Hebrew Israelite Group," *New York Times*, December 11, 2019, https://www.nytimes.com/2019/12/11/nyregion/jersey-city-shooting.html#link-76d85db4.

36 Cited in D. Mackenzie, T. Falcon, and J. Rahman, eds., *Religion Gone Astray: What We Found at the Heart of Interfaith* (Woodstock, VT: Skylight Paths, 2011), 21.

37 Saul Jay Singer, "The Anti-Semitism of George Bernard Shaw," Jewish Press, May 6, 2015, https://www.jewishpress.com/sections/features/features-on-jewish-world/the-anti-semitism-of-george-bernard-shaw/2015/05/06/.

slandered as an imposter or deemed unworthy. They are mocked as arrogant for daring to claim a special status that all other faiths claim for themselves. And they are held in contempt for scriptural words in books that Christians and Muslims also regard as holy. Amid all the noise and fury, the Jew seems to plod onward in their mission perhaps slightly bemused that the words of the Hebrew Bible should so animate those who clearly dislike the Hebrew.

Money

Postcard of the propaganda exhibition "The Eternal Jew" in 1937, Horst Schlüter (pseudonym). Public domain, via Wikimedia Commons

> "What is the worldly religion of the Jew? Huckstering.
> What is his worldly God? Money.....
> Money is the jealous god of Israel,
> in face of which no other god may exist.
> Money degrades all the gods of man—and
> turns them into commodities....
> The bill of exchange is the real god of the Jew."[1]
>
> —Karl Marx

Of all the growths that cling to the Jew, the association with money is surely the most visible. It is to be found in high literature and political manifestos, crude remarks, even misplaced compliments. It is the slur with which individual Jews are most likely to have been confronted, most likely to have personally felt. It can be said that every Jew, without exception, has personally felt the sting of the remark about the rich Jew or the stingy Jew.

The British writer Howard Jacobson observed that "'you Jewed me' was common schoolyard usage in Manchester right up to 1960 and, for all I know, beyond." It was equally common in schoolyards in Sydney in the 1990s. As Jacobson notes, "whatever pain was caused by it, offence was rarely intended,"[2] so common had it become.

---

1   Karl Marx, "On the Jewish Question" (1844), in Enzo Traverso, *The Jewish Question: History of a Marxist Debate* (Leiden: Brill, 2018), 17.

2   Howard Jacobson, "Myth Busting: Are Jews Actually Rich? From Judas to the Brick Lane Mural, How the Malicious Libel about Jewish Greed Gripped the Global Imagination," *New Statesman*, April 17, 2019, https://www.newstatesman.com/culture/2019/04/jews-and-the-money-myth.

In December 2021, an associate professor at the Ohio State University was recorded in a lecture describing her experience of bargaining in Mexico as "Jewing people down."[3] In issuing a statement of apology, the professor made the admission, incredible yet indicative, that she "never associated the word 'jew' with any person or group." This defense is worthy of closer examination. The professor, presumably earnestly, never thought of a Jewish person when using the word "Jew." This is because the term "Jew" had undergone a sort of mitosis, a splitting off, whereby it at is once a noun meaning a Jewish person, a verb meaning to swindle or haggle, and an adjective describing a shady handler of money. This process was centuries in the making. *The Oxford English Dictionary* from 1933, included the following entry for "Jew": "1. Jew: trans. and offensive. As a name of opprobrium: spec. applied to a grasping or extortionate person."[4]

These incidents may give the impression of childish stereotype, a mere nuisance. Yet the harm caused by the myth of the moneyed or stingy Jew is not confined to the giving of offence at dinner parties or the occasional misstep by an academic. It has contributed to a certain perception of Jews that has fed into some of the most virulent and deadly antisemitic myths—the Jew as controller of global finance, the Jew as

---

3   Rachel Hale, "Students Demand Further Action after Ohio State Professor Says 'Jewing people down' in Class Lecture," Forward, December 23, 2021, https://forward.com/fast-forward/479958/students-demand-further-action-after-ohio-state-professor-says-jewing/.

4   Sara Lipton, "A Terribly Durable Myth, Review of the Exhibition 'Jews, Money, Myth' at the Jewish Museum in London," *New York Review of Books*, June 27, 2019, https://www.nybooks.com/articles/2019/06/27/jews-money-terribly-durable-myth/?lp_txn_id=1309236.

cunning and untrustworthy, the Jew as motivated by the evil inclination, and the Jew as the obstacle to a better, less materialistic, more spiritual world.

The origins of the association of Jews with money are ancient and complex. One could point to the betrayal of Jesus by his disciple Judas for thirty pieces of silver. This is but one of history's examples of grand betrayal—Benedict Arnold offered West Point to the British in return for 20,000 pounds, Quisling and Petain handed over their countries to the Nazis, Brutus betrayed the greatest hero of Roman history. Yet nowhere has this caused an entire people to be associated, racially and perennially, with the crimes of these infamous individuals. But in the case of Judas, the victim is the Christ, and the greedy betrayer bears the name of his nation. As Joan Acocella notes, "almost since the death of Christ, Judas has been held up by Christians as a symbol of the Jews: their supposed deviousness, their lust for money."[5]

Judas may explain an early association of Jews with the evil pursuit of money, but it is in the Europe of the Middle Ages that the identification became deeply ingrained. As we have seen, both Christianity and Islam sought to maintain the Jews in a position of servility and inferiority, so that the idea that the Jews had been surpassed, were spiritually blind to the divinity of Jesus and Mohammed and were being punished by God for it, became self-fulfilling.

---

5   Joan Acocella, "Betrayal: Should We Hate Judas Iscariot?," *New Yorker*, July 27, 2009, https://www.newyorker.com/magazine/2009/08/03/betrayal-2.

Papal edicts from the thirteenth century had banned Jews from guilds thereby preventing them from working in trades or as merchants, fields in which the Jews had traditionally excelled and to which they were drawn. They had been barred from public office and from holding academic degrees, limiting their options further still. Pope Paul IV's edict on July 14, 1555 titled "Cum Nimis Absurdum" or "Since it is absurd," decreed that "Jews are to be limited to the trade of rag-picking and they cannot trade in grain, barley or any other commodity essential to human welfare."[6] The spirit in which these papal laws were enacted was clear from Pope Paul's preamble: "… instead of the slavery, which they deserve, they manage to claim superiority: we, who recently learned that these very Jews have insolently invaded Rome from a number of the Papal States, territories and domains, to the extent that not only have they mingled with Christians (even when close to their churches) and wearing no identifying garments …"

Since Jews could not live off their skills, work with their tools or aspire to the university or to public life, they were left to commercialize money itself. The lending of money for interest, usury, had become off-limits to Christians after the Third Lateran Council of 1179 enacted a proposal of Pope Alexander III to punish usury with excommunication.[7]

---

6   Pope Paul IV, "Cum Nimis Absurdum," July 14, 1555, https://www.ccjr.us/dialogika-resources/primary-texts-from-the-history-of-the-relationship/paul-iv.

7   Nathan Dorn, "The Consilia of Alessandro Nievo: On Jews and Usury in 15th-Century Italy," May 20, 2016, https://blogs.loc.gov/law/2016/05/the-consilia-of-alessandro-nievo-on-jews-and-usury-in-15th-century-italy/.

Naturally, all of this ensured that the Jews came more and more to moneylending. It was virtually the last path open to them, it was always in demand, and easily transferable to other towns and countries. It would also be disastrous for the Jews, placing a people considered inferior in the position of creditor, and leaving them open to despicable acts of treachery and exploitation.

The attitude of Jews to moneylending was complex. Other ancient peoples had recognized the commercial necessity of money lending for an expanding, settled society and the legitimacy of charging interest owing to the risks inherent in lending. These other peoples therefore freely permitted it.

The Jews took a more considered attitude. Predatory lending, extortionate rates of interest, surrender of property, living in fear of being ruined by the lender, remain features of the money trade to this day. The ancient Jews recognized the inevitability of such practices, and what they could to the fragile bonds of community. Lending with interest was therefore prohibited unless one was lending to a stranger.

Deuteronomy 23:19 made the position clear: "Do not charge a fellow Israelite interest, whether on money or food or anything else that may earn interest." The laws were constantly being adapted like modern tax codes; loopholes were closed as they were discovered. But the law further provided that "you may charge a foreigner interest, but not a fellow Israelite, so that the Lord your God may bless you in everything you put your hand to in the land you are entering to possess."[8]

---

8   Book of Deuteronomy 23:19.

This law made sense when Jews lived as a settled society in their own homeland. For a Jew settled in Judea to charge interest to a passing merchant or a foreign traveller was entirely reasonable. But could it be justified when the Jews lived as minorities in the countries of others?

The Jews realized that how they interpreted this law in their exile, would reverberate for centuries to come. They faced poverty without moneylending but even deeper hatred with it. So before turning to the money trade, they turned to their rabbinical authorities for clarity. Philo argued that as the Jews now lived among the nations and not in their own homeland, the non-Jews in their midst could not be considered strangers. The prohibition on interest would therefore need to be extended to all countrymen, not merely fellow Jews. The inhospitality with which the Jews were treated, the breadth of laws enacted to impoverish and demean them made it much easier to argue the contrary position. If the host nation most certainly considered Jews strangers and not countrymen, why shouldn't the Jews reciprocate? Thus, Philo's opinion became a dissenting one. The prevailing view was that "if we nowadays allow interest to be taken from non-Jews it is because there is no end to the yoke and burden kings and ministers impose on us."[9]

Faced with the wretched choice of usury or impoverishment, the Jews chose the former, and in doing so, spawned an association that would torment them through the centuries.

We might rationalize that moneylending was and remains a necessary aspect of commerce and that the contract to borrow

---

9   Talmud, Tos. to BM 70b s.v. *tashikh*.

and repay with interest is freely entered into. But consider the dynamics it created between Jews and non-Jews. Christians now found themselves in the debt of people they had been told were inferior to them. In the event of default, Jews now had legal cause to pursue Christians and seize their property including hereditary estates. More so, this relationship became virtually the only form of contact that Jews and non-Jews ever had. The papal decree of "Cum Nimis Absurdum" also prescribed that "Jews may not presume in any way to play, eat or fraternize with Christians" and "they are not to be addressed as superiors [even] by poor Christians." Thus, the interaction between Jews and Christians came to be almost exclusively in the realm of money, interest and indebtedness. From this, the association between Jews and money was permanently forged.

More and more Jews turned to moneylending. As Paul Johnson noted, one rabbi with knowledge of both the French and Italian Jewish communities wrote that in the second half of the fifteenth century, the Jews there hardly engaged in any other profession.[10]

Writing of the Jews of the French region of Alsace, the historian I. H. Hirsch observed that usury had not made them wealthy at the expense of others, rather it deepened their misery:

> Practically the towns were hermetically sealed against them. They might only dwell in the villages, and in them moneylending

10 Paul Johnson, *A History of the Jews* (London: Weidenfeld and Nicolson, 1987), 174.

was unhappily the only pursuit to which they might devote their intellect and their industry; and even in that the restrictions were so comprehensive and the administration of the law so completely in the hands of ill-wishers that every loan they made was almost irrecoverable if the debtor were inclined to refuse payment. As a consequence, their poverty and degradation could hardly reach a lower depth.[11]

There were of course reasons beyond compulsion and necessity that drew Jews to finance. Money is fungible, portable and always valued. For a people who had to routinely ransom themselves or their community leaders in cases of extortion and arbitrary arrest, who often had to bribe chieftains or police captains to protect them from the mob, who were used to fleeing when word of a pogrom or crusader raid was heard, the money business made sense. Certainly, more sense than the trade of commercial goods, agriculture, from which they were barred anyway, but that also lacked both mobility and liquidity. It may have also given the Jews a false hope of uplift in the eyes of their hosts. Perhaps they thought they would be regarded as financiers, serious men of business.

The Jews were not the only people in Europe engaged in moneylending. Why else would it have been necessary for the pope to decree to his subjects that usury would result in excommunication? A law passed in Florence in 1406 stated

---

11   I. H. Hersch, "French Revolution and the Emancipation of the Jews," *Jewish Quarterly Review* 19, no. 3 (1907): 544.

that "the Jews are enemies of the cross, of our Lord Jesus Christ, and of all Christians, and that they engage in usury against the mandate of God's Holy Church."[12] And yet the large Christian banking houses that dominated the economy continued to profit from the taking of interest.[13] What is permitted the host is denied to the despised interloper.

The indebtedness to the Jews fomented a loathing at every level of society. From clergymen who saw the Jews acquiring wealth and so rising from their lowly station, to the worker who took on excessive debt, and the nobility who bitterly resented the special protections afforded the Jews as sources of great revenue for the ruling class. They came to be reviled more and more.

Pope Clement VII charged that "all the world suffers from the usury of the Jews, their monopolies and deceit. They have brought many unfortunate peoples into a state of poverty, especially farmers, working-class people, and the very poor." *The Domesday Book* recorded that "The ostentation which possession of great wealth enabled the Jews to display, made them an object of universal dislike; as usurers."[14]

It was inevitable that the Jewish involvement with moneylending would end disastrously. In medieval England, by 1200, the Jews "began to occupy an economic niche as

---

12 A. Gow and G. Griffiths, "Pope Eugenius IV and Jewish Money-Lending in Florence: The Case of Salomone di Bonaventura during the Chancellorship of Leonardo Bruni," *Renaissance Quarterly 47*, no. 2 (1994): 282–329.

13 Ibid.

14 Austin Lane Poole, *The Oxford History of England: From Domesday Book to Magna Carta 1087–1216* (Oxford: Clarendon Press, 1951), 353.

moneylenders and enjoyed a virtual monopoly in the practice for the next fifty years."[15] Rather than seeking to prohibit Jewish moneylending, the king instead regulated it in order to draw profits for the ruling class, by establishing an Exchequer of the Jewry through which all transactions could be monitored and taxed. In this way, the Crown enabled the practice to flourish and lined royal coffers while remaining at arm's length from the dirty business itself. In York, in 1190, the entire Jewish community was burned alive or forced into mass suicide as a mob incited by barons in the debt of Jewish moneylenders turned the masses upon the Jews. The apparent motive for the devastation was to destroy logs recording debts owed to Jewish moneylenders.[16]

As mob violence escalated and the presence of Jewish moneylenders drew ever greater outrage from the barons and knights, the king was faced with an almighty conundrum: ban the practice and forfeit a lucrative means of indirectly taxing the masses or continue to protect moneylending and risk the wrath of the people. To make matters even more interesting, "the king's court was awash in moneylending and his family was deeply implicated in its consequences."[17]

The king announced the termination of the "heinous practice" of lending for interest for its "abasement of our people."[18] By edict of July 18, 1290, the Jews of England were expelled.

---

15   Mark Koyama, "The Political Economy of Expulsion: The Regulation of Jewish Moneylending in Medieval England," *Constitutional Political Economy 21*, no. 4 (2010): 380.

16   Ibid., 382.

17   Ibid., 394.

18   Ibid., 396.

First, their money and other assets were simply taken from them in what proved a disappointing haul. The extent of Jewish accumulation of wealth was grossly exaggerated, even then. In exchange for issuing the expulsion edict, his parliament granted the king an enormous tax on wool allowing him to be rid of the Jew while keeping up his revenue.

As can be observed with all antisemitic myths, what was conceived by a sinister few then reached the masses through art and literature.

The character of Fagin in Charles Dickens's *Oliver Twist* exploited and coerced orphan children to steal at his behest growing rich through exploitation and deviancy. There is Meyer Wolfsheim in F. Scott Fitzgerald's *The Great Gatsby*, who fixed the World Series, defiling the national pastime for money, a man who could "play with the faith of fifty million people— with the single-mindedness of a burglar blowing a safe."

It is true that at least the characters of Fagin and Wolfsheim were based on real people. Fagin is said to be based on Ikey Solomon, a British criminal sent to the Australian penal colony for receiving stolen goods. Wolfsheim is based on Arnold Rothstein, who is reputed to have fixed the 1919 World Series. But Solomon was an oddity in large part because he was one of very few Jewish convicts, not because his conduct was indicative of his nation. Rothstein was an audacious, cold-blooded hoodlum but his exploits were no different to non-Jewish mobsters and crime syndicates who routinely fixed prize fights, world cups and other major sporting events. Yet when a dramatic role called for a shady, unscrupulous money manipulator, invariably that character would be made a Jew.

The association has become so automatic that it is often made unwittingly. A play by the British playwright Al Smith, titled "Rare Earth Mettle" and performed at the Royal Theatre in London in 2021, featured a leading character with the unmistakably Jewish name, Hershel Fink. He is described as "a narcissistic, egomaniacal tech mogul who dances around the stage in expensive tracksuits, manipulating people, geography and grief for his own gain, too rich to care about anything."[19] When challenged on why the character, who was not Jewish, was given an obviously Jewish name that aligned with an obvious Jewish stereotype, the theatre claimed "unconscious bias."[20] If taken at face value, just like the professor who never imaged that "jewing down" might be offensive, or even relate to Jews, this is further evidence that the association of Jews and money is so hardwired it barely engages the conscious mind.

The depiction of Shylock in Shakespeare's "The Merchant of Venice" is literature's most powerful portrayal of the Jew as underhanded, money-centric and lusting to exact vengeance upon good Christians. Its significance lies in the striking vitality of the character, whose qualities tower over all else in an otherwise mediocre play by Shakespeare's standards. Shylock has graced theatres and school curricula for hundreds of years. The novelist Philip Roth held it to be the very source of Jew-hatred. In Roth's novel *Operation Shylock*, published in 1993, Roth argues that the fate of the Jews was sealed in three words,

---

19   Kate Wyver, "Rare Earth Mettle Review—Secret Deals and Wordy Debates," *Guardian*, November 17, 2021, https://www.theguardian.com/stage/2021/nov/17/rare-earth-mettle-review-secret-deals-and-wordy-debates.

20   Ibid.

the opening line given to Shylock by the Bard. "Three words," Roth writes, "by which the savage, repellent and villainous Jew, deformed by hatred and revenge, entered as our doppelganger into the consciousness of the enlightened West. You remember the three words? What Jew can forget them? What Christian can forgive them? 'Three thousand ducats.'"

"The Merchant of Venice" is the story of a Jewish moneylender who seeks to take a pound of flesh from the chest of a Christian debtor who has long tormented and mocked him, when the debt cannot be repaid. It has been criticized as a work of antisemitism, but it can also be seen as representing the world as it is and not necessarily as Shakespeare wanted it to be. Shylock is ultimately defeated, humiliated, and loses his daughter who elopes with one of Shylock's foes. As we have seen in the case of the use and disposal of the Jews of England, in medieval Europe, the Jew always lost. They scrambled and made do, carved out an existence, but they were always wholly expendable and at the mercy of others.

The humiliating manner of Shylock's defeat is also in keeping with the treatment of Jews in medieval Italy at the hands of their Christian neighbors. As Paul Johnson records, in Turin, students had the right to pelt Jews with snowballs upon the first fall of winter snow unless they paid a ransom of twenty-five ducats. In Pisa, there existed a tradition on the feast of St Catherine whereby the students would put the city's fattest Jew on the scales and made the community pay a fine equal to his weight in sweets.[21] Why would Shylock fare any better in sixteenth-century Venice?

---

21 Johnson, A History of the Jews, 214.

What's more, the most famous lines of the play, the most powerful rhetoric, belong not to the Christians but to Shylock. Few will quote any other lines from the play than,

> I am a Jew. Hath not a Jew eyes? Hath not a Jew hands, organs, dimensions, senses, affections, passions? Fed with the same food, hurt with the same weapons, subject to the same diseases, healed by the same means, warmed and cooled by the same winter and summer as a Christian is? If you prick us, do we not bleed? If you tickle us, do we not laugh? If you poison us, do we not die? And if you wrong us, shall we not revenge?[22]

And while the Venetian playboys leave Shylock trounced, they are hardly endearing figures. The greatest wisdom in the play belongs to Shylock too. He tells the court:

> If you deny me, fie upon your law!
> There is no force in the decrees of Venice.
> I stand for judgment: answer; shall I have it?[23]

Shakespeare's intentions can be debated but never known. But to most readers, particularly schoolchildren to whom the text is assigned in high schools around the world, it presents as an uncomplicated tale of Jewish greed and vengeance pitted

---

22 William Shakespeare, "The Merchant of Venice," Act 3 Scene I.
23 Ibid., Act 4 Scene I.

against good Christian folk. It is a simple hero story where the villain is a hideous Jew. The reading of "The Merchant of Venice" in a classroom in Sydney in the late 1990s certainly yielded cheers of delight when Shylock the Jew loses everything.

The image of the moneyed, stingy Jew is not merely the stuff of crass stereotypes and schoolyard mockery. It also implicates the Jews not only in accumulating and hoarding great wealth but using these gains for subversive ends.

Karl Marx saw the Jew as the arch-capitalist, the obstacle to the solidarity of labor. Martin Luther saw the Jews as the enemies of Christianity, the obstacles to a world of goodly spirituality. In private letters, Marx wrote of "Jewish niggers" and "Jewish moneygrubbers."[24]

Luther called the Jews a "base and whoring people" full of the "devil's faeces . . . they wallow in like swine." In his pamphlet "On the Jews and their Lies," he urged, "first their synagogues should be set on fire, and whatever is left should be buried in dirt so that no one may ever be able to see a stone or cinder of it. Jewish prayer-books should be destroyed and rabbis be forbidden to preach. Then the Jewish people should be dealt with, their homes smashed and destroyed and their inmates put under one roof or in a stable like gypsies, to teach them they are not masters in our land."[25]

---

24 William H. Blanchard, "Karl Marx and the Jewish Question," *Political Psychology* 5, no. 3 (1984): 366–367.

25 Dorothea Wendebourg, "Martin Luther, Jews, and Judaism," *Oxford Research Encyclopedia of Religion*, March 29, 2017.

Elsewhere in the pamphlet Luther wrote of "thieving," "murderous" usurers to be "hunted down, cursed and beheaded." Luther called the Jews "thirsty bloodhounds and murderers of all Christendom."

Luther's program for dealing with the Jews was meticulously implemented by the Nazis. Indeed, the burning of the synagogues that Luther had commanded took place in 1938, beginning in the early hours of November 10, Luther's birthday, in what came to be known as the night of broken glass or *Kristallnacht*. The significance of this was not lost on the Nazis or their supporters.

The Bishop of the Evangelical Church of Thuringia, Martin Sasse, who weeks later published a pamphlet titled *Martin Luther and the Jews: Away with Them!* wrote, "On 10 November, Luther's birthday, the synagogues are burning … At this moment, we must hear the voice of the prophet of the Germans from the sixteenth century, who out of ignorance began as a friend of the Jews but who, guided by his conscience, experience and reality became the greatest antisemite of his age, the one who warned his nation against the Jews."[26]

Luther and Marx expressed their antisemitism through their reforming economic and religious movements. As the movements grew, the myth of Jews and money grew with it.

In March 2018, Jeremy Corbyn, the former leader of British Labour initially criticized the removal of a mural in London which depicted hook-nosed bankers playing monopoly on the backs of the masses. In February 2019, Minnesota

---

26 Noam Marans, "On Luther and his Lies," American Jewish Committee, October 11, 2017, https://www.ajc.org/news/on-luther-and-his-lies.

Congresswoman Ilhan Omar suggested that pro-Israel groups were essentially paying US politicians to support Israel,[27] initially defending her remarks as a critique of lobbying power. In both cases, the target and the insinuation were the same—Jews and their money.

While not mentioning the Jews by name, in a speech in March 2018, the Hungarian President Viktor Orban invoked powerful themes of Jewish money corrupting democracy and undermining the national interest. "They do not fight directly, but by stealth," he said. "They are not honourable, but unprincipled; they are not national, but international; they do not believe in work, but speculate with money; they have no homeland, but feel that the whole world is theirs. They are not generous, but vengeful, and always attack the heart—especially if it is red, white and green [the colors of the Hungarian flag]."[28]

The image of the moneyed Jew often takes the form of presumed business acumen or a reference to Jewish wealth and success. Still today, market stalls in Krakow and Warsaw in Poland are full of little figurines depicting Orthodox Jews with pouches of money or gold coins.[29]

27   Emily Burack, "Ilhan Omar's Anti-Semitism Controversy, Explained," Jewish Telegraphic Agency, February 14, 2019, https://www.jta.org/2019/02/14/politics/the-ilhan-omar-anti-semitism-controversy-explained.

28   Erna Paris, "Viktor Orban's War on George Soros and Hungary's Jews," *Globe and Mail*, June 1, 2018, https://www.theglobeandmail.com/opinion/article-viktor-orbans-war-on-george-soros-and-hungarys-jews/.

29   Ilana Belfer, "Hey Poland, What's Up with Those Lucky Jew Statues?," Vice, October 10, 2013, https://www.vice.com/en/article/qbnewm/hey-poland-whats-up-with-those-lucky-jew-statues.

In 2018, the basketball superstar Lebron James posted a video to Instagram in which he sang the lyrics of a rap song. The lyrics were, "we be getting that Jewish money, everything is kosher." At the time, James had a following of over 45 million users. James eventually apologized explaining, "I actually thought it was a compliment."[30] More "unconscious bias."

We might consider these as benign, light-hearted stereotypes but they serve to normalize a dangerous prejudice and reinforce the connection between a people and a commodity seen as the root of all kinds of evil.[31] Incitement of mob violence against the Jews was made easier by the spreading of rumors that even the most impoverished Jews hid gold or currency on their person.

Antisemitism has often been conveyed euphemistically or through what is commonly referred to as "dog-whistles." It would immediately strike the ear as hateful to refer to Jewish control of banks or of Jews manipulating the money markets for their own malevolent ends. Instead, by invoking the Rothschild banking dynasty or substituting "Jew" for "Zionist," the same statements appear as political observations, perhaps even insights. As William Korey noted in his paper on Stalinist antisemitism, "the collective Jew has been redefined as the "Zionist."[32]

---

30 Ben Rohrbach, "LeBron James Apologizes for Sharing Anti-Semitic Song Lyrics on Instagram," Yahoo Sports, December 25, 2018, https://au.sports.yahoo.com/lebron-james-apologizes-sharing-anti-semitic-song-lyrics-instagram-155131217.html.

31 1 Timothy 6:10.

32 William Korey, "The Origins and Development of Soviet Anti-Semitism: An Analysis," *Slavic Review* 31, no. 1 (1972): 111–135. https://doi.org/10.2307/2494148.

Despite the coded language, such statements are, all the same, steeped in perceptions of Jewish greed and financial manipulation. Mirroring Marx's antisemitic pronouncements, Soviet propaganda charged that "Zionism is the lackey at the beck and call of the rich master whose nationality is exploitation and whose God is the dollar."[33]

The Nation of Islam leader Louis Farrakhan frequently sermonizes on these themes, effortlessly toggling between open attacks on the Jews and what must appear to his followers to be enlightened observations about the unseen hand.

In a speech at the Mosque Maryam in Chicago in 2010, Farrakhan demonstrated how terms like "Rothschild," "Jew" and "Zionist" become interchangeable in antisemitic discourse. "The Federal Reserve is a group of Jewish and gentile bankers that took over the printing of your money," Farrakhan declared. "It's not U.S.-government owned, it's a family of Jewish and gentile international bankers, the head of whom is the Rothschild family. These bankers know that only in war will America have to borrow money... This is why they were upset with Jack Kennedy, he wanted to come out of Vietnam. And they killed him, I believe."[34]

Following a devastating fire in the Grenfell Tower public housing block in London, Nazim Ali, a director of the Islamic Human Rights Commission (IHRC), addressed a rally just days after the tragedy and declared to an already enraged audience, "As we know in Grenfell, many innocents were murdered by Theresa May's cronies, many of which are supporters

33 Ibid.
34 Farrakhan, speech at Mosque Maryam.

of Zionist ideology … Let us not forget that some of the biggest corporations who have supported the Conservative Party are Zionists."[35]

A woman volunteering at the site of the fire, Tahra Ahmed, alleged that the Grenfell tower victims were "burned alive in a Jewish sacrifice," that "Jews have always been the ones behind ritual torture, crucifixion and murder of children, especially young boys,"[36] and that both the tower fire and 9/11 attacks were motivated by supposedly Jewish property owners seeking insurance proceeds: "Just like the twin towers was owned by Jew Silverstein who collected trillions in insurance claims."[37] Ahmed's posts appeared in a Facebook group with over fifty-five thousand members.[38]

Two brutal murders in Paris show just how dangerous the perception of the moneyed Jew continues to be. In November 2021, Yacine Mihoub was convicted of stabbing eighty-five-year-old Mireille Knoll eleven times and then setting her body alight during an attempted robbery in her home. Knoll lived next door to Mihoub's mother, and she had acted as a surrogate grandmother to her killer when he was a child. Mihoub

---

35   Rory Tingle, "Islamic Activist Causes Outrage after Claiming Grenfell Towers Victims 'were murdered' by 'Zionists who fund the Tories,'" *Daily Mail*, July 10, 2017, https://www.dailymail.co.uk/news/article-4679988/Islamic-activist-blames-Zionists-Grenfell-Tower-fire.html.

36   "Grenfell Volunteer who Said Blaze was 'Jewish Sacrifice' Convicted of Stirring Up Racial Hatred," *Jewish Chronicle*, January 14, 2022, https://www.thejc.com/news/news/grenfell-volunteer-who-said-blaze-was-jewish-sacrifice-convicted-of-stirring-up-racial-hatred-6ARwYYN-yohTnuJ73c088Ok.

37   Ibid.

38   Ibid.

and his accomplice believed that their victim, who had survived deportations of Parisian Jews to the death camps, had "hidden treasures" in her home.[39] Mihoub's accomplice had said, "she's a Jew. She must have money."

In February 2006, Ilan Halimi, a twenty-three-year-old mobile phone salesman who lived with his mother in public housing was found naked with his head shaved, handcuffed and covered with burn marks and stab wounds near rail tracks, in the southern Paris suburb of Sainte-Genevieve-des-Bois. In a state of shock and unable to speak, he died on the way to hospital. He had been held, tortured and beaten for three weeks, his head wrapped in tape, eyes sellotaped shut and fed through a straw, while a gang known as the Barbarians demanded a ransom from his family.[40] The ringleader, Yousouff Fofana, had instructed his accomplices to target Jews for ransom kidnappings. "They are loaded with money," he told them.[41]

39 "Mireille Knoll: Killer of French Holocaust Survivor Jailed for Life," BBC, November 10, 2021, https://www.bbc.com/news/world-europe-59239981.

40 Angelique Chrisafis, "Trial Opens into Alleged Gang Kidnap, Torture and Murder of French Jew," *Guardian*, April 30, 2009, https://www.theguardian.com/world/2009/apr/29/torture-murder-anti-semitism-trial-france.

41 "French Gang on Trial over Harrowing Murder of Jewish Man," France24, April 28, 2009, https://www.france24.com/en/20090428-french-gang-trial-over-harrowing-murder-jewish-man-.

MYTH 6

Dual Loyalties

Illustration from a 1919 Austrian postcard showing a caricatured Jew
stabbing a personified German Army soldier in the back with a dagger.
Public domain, via Wikimedia Commons

> "Must one admit into the family a tribe that constantly turns its eyes toward another homeland?"[1]
>
> —Bishop of Clancy

On September 26, 1894, French Intelligence intercepted a message believed to be from an artillery officer on the general staff of the French army. The message contained classified information that was being sent to the German military attaché, Lieutenant-Colonel von Schwartzkoppen. Among the classified information passed to the Germans were details of new weaponry being developed by the French. The discovery two years later of further leaked communications matched the handwriting of the original intercepted message, revealing the traitor to almost certainly be Ferdinand Walsin Esterhazy.

Esterhazy was an infantry major of dubious repute, frequently in debt, who once tried to swindle his own nephew using forged documents. He was eventually turfed out of the army on the charge of "habitual misconduct." Nevertheless, Esterhazy was not immediately suspected.

When the leak to the Germans was discovered, an investigation was conducted, which established that the culprit could only be one of half a dozen possible officers who had access to the classified information. One of the suspects was Captain Alfred Dreyfus, a career soldier with an unblemished record. Dreyfus had been motivated to serve in the military from a

---

1 The French National Assembly, "Debate on the Eligibility of Jews for Citizenship" (December 23, 1789), in *The Jew in the Modern World*, ed. P. R. Mendes-Flohr and J. Reinharz (New York: Oxford University Press, 1995), 116.

young age after witnessing the misery caused by the Franco-Prussian War in 1870. He was also the only Jew on the general staff. He was soon arrested.

Colonel Sandherr, commander of the French military's counter-espionage service, sent a message to the French Foreign Minister that the traitor had been apprehended: "The officer charged with treason is a Jew," Sandherr remarked, "… his false and conceited character, in which one recognizes all the pride and all the ignominy of his race, have made him suspect for a long time."[2]

Following his arrest, Dreyfus was tried, convicted and court-martialled on the charge of high treason. In the courtyard of the École Militaire in Paris, a warrant-officer cut off the badges and buttons from Dreyfus's military dress, then removed the ceremonial sword from his scabbard and snapped it across his knee. All the while Dreyfus professed his innocence and shouted, "long live France! Long live the Army!" Dreyfus was then deported and incarcerated in solitary confinement on the treacherous Devil's Island.

The trial of Dreyfus was conducted in closed session, but a leak from the military headquarters to the publisher of an antisemitic newspaper soon ensured the public was made aware that a Jewish officer stood accused of treason against the French Republic. As Dreyfus was paraded around the court-yard like a captured slave of Rome, a crowd of Frenchmen

---

2   Louis Begley, *Why the Dreyfus Affair Matters* (New Haven: Yale University Press, 2009), published in extract form in the *Washington Post*, October 11, 2009.

had gathered and chanted, "Death to Dreyfus!" and "Death to Jews!"[3]

The "Dreyfus Affair" is most commonly associated with the legal principle of miscarriage of justice and historically with the story of Zionism and the creation of the modern State of Israel. Theodor Herzl, regarded as the founding father of modern Zionism, had been sent to report on the trial as a journalist and he witnessed Dreyfus's debasement. He concluded from the spectacle that even the most patriotic, assimilated European Jew was not safe from antisemitism and that a national homeland could alone deliver the Jews from the hardships and their perils that awaited them. But the "Dreyfus Affair" is significant for another reason. It serves as a leading example of the belief in inherent Jewish disloyalty.

The term, "dual loyalties" conveys a splitting of allegiances, an inner conflict where one is torn between two different, sometimes incompatible affiliations. Many ethnic groups have had their loyalties questioned and have been subjected to suspicion particularly in times of conflict. In the United States, Americans of Japanese extraction were infamously interned in camps amid suspicion that they would aid the enemy following the Japanese attack on Pearl Harbor. The syndicated journalist Westbrook Pegler claimed that "the Japanese in California should be under armed guard to the last man and woman right now …"[4] Australians of German, Italian and

---

3   Johnson, *A History of the Jews*, 380.
4   "Japanese American Incarceration," The National World War II Museum, New Orleans, https://www.nationalww2museum.org/war/articles/japanese-american-incarceration.

Japanese background were also interned.[5] Rising tensions between China and the United States have also fuelled "scrutiny of Chinese-Americans and people of Chinese descent."[6]

Yet the dual loyalty accusation is applied in an altogether different manner when it comes to the Jews. The suspicion that Jews are foremost loyal to the State of Israel above the countries in which they have lived, often for generations, is not the product of wartime paranoia or a slack racism rearing in turbulent times. It is a permanent condition that is derived not from external events but from the imputed nature of the Jew.

More than a century before the trial of Alfred Dreyfus, France had debated whether to emancipate its Jewish population and grant them equal rights as French citizens. On September 27, 1791 the National Assembly, the French legislative body during the French Revolution, voted in favor of emancipation but only after a clamorous, divisive public debate.

A radical left-wing deputy from Alsace bitterly opposed equality for the Jews whom he referred to as "cruel hordes of Africans who had infested my region."[7] Another member of the National Assembly, Stanislas de Clermont-Tonnerre, argued in favor of emancipation. "The Jews should be denied

---

5 "Wartime Internment Camps in Australia," National Archives of Australia, https://www.naa.gov.au/explore-collection/immigration-and-citizenship/wartime-internment-camps-australia.

6 Russell Flannery, "Chinese-American Groups Trying to Push Back against Loyalty Tests, Discrimination," Forbes, October 3, 2019, https://www.forbes.com/sites/russellflannery/2019/10/03/chinese-american-groups-trying-to-push-back-against-loyalty-tests-discrimination/?sh=129e6fc11ce4.

7 Johnson, *A History of the Jews*, 306.

everything as a nation," he said, "but granted everything as individuals."[8]

Napoleon's conquests emancipated the Jews beyond France and afforded them the freedom, at least in law, to live as equal citizens and participate in wider society. Napoleon liberated many of the ghettoes of Italy, lifted prohibitions on the construction of synagogues and granted them full and equal rights. The fact that this was done rapidly by decree of a foreign conqueror no doubt left a festering resentment, but it also enabled the Jews to finally emerge from within ghetto walls and begin to interact with their countrymen and pierce the mythology that had enveloped them.

For all the rights Napoleon granted to the Jews, he was nevertheless dubious as to what the Jews actually were as a people and how they would behave as free citizens. In 1806, he convened an Assembly of Jewish Notables consisting of 111 Jewish leaders, to serve as a consultative body on the integration of Jews. The Notables were posed twelve questions by the emperor, through which he could seek to determine whether Jews were truly capable of integration or whether their customs and beliefs destined them to remain a nation within a nation.

Two of the questions concerned usury. Seven of the questions probed Jewish custom and administration including the appointment of rabbis, marriage laws and the settlement of internal disputes. A further three questions went to the heart of the dual loyalty accusation. These questions sought

---

8   Lynn Hunt, trans., *The French Revolution and Human Rights: A Brief Documentary History* (Boston/New York: Bedford/St. Martin's, 1996), 86–88.

to determine whether the Jews could function as French citizens or if Voltaire's summation of the Jews was correct and they possessed "a violent hatred of all those nations which have tolerated them,"[9] which made them unfit and unworthy of emancipation.

The Jewish Notables were asked: "In the eyes of Jews, are Frenchmen considered as their brethren? Or are they considered as strangers? What line of conduct does their law prescribe towards Frenchmen not of their religion? Do Jews born in France, and treated by the laws as French citizens, consider France their country? Are they bound to defend it? Are they bound to obey the laws and to conform to the dispositions of the civil code?"[10]

The lucidity of the answers would have surprised many who had long been led to believe that the Jews were an unrefined and backward people. The responses reveal that the Jewish leaders were enthusiastic to please, giving precise, unequivocal responses that could not be distorted or maliciously misconstrued. Their answers also left no doubt about Jewish loyalties and how they viewed their countrymen:

> In the eyes of Jews, Frenchmen are their brethren, and are not strangers. When the Israelites settled land or formed an independent nation, their law made it a rule for them to consider

---

9 Haim Hillel Ben-Sasson, *A History of the Jewish People* (Cambridge, MA: Harvard University Press, 1985), 745.

10 The Assembly of Jewish Notables, Answers to Napoleon, http://people.ucalgary.ca/~elsegal/363_Transp/Sanhedrin.html.

strangers as their brethren. With the most tender care for their welfare, their lawgiver commands to love them, "Love ye therefore the strangers," says he to the Israelites, "for ye were strangers in the "land of Egypt." Respect and benevolence towards strangers are enforced by Moses, not as an exhortation to the practice of social morality only, but as an obligation imposed by God himself.

A religion whose fundamental maxims are such—a religion which makes a duty of loving the stranger—which enforces the practice of social virtues, must surely require that its followers should consider their fellow-citizens as brethren.

And how could they consider them otherwise when they inhabit the same land, when they are ruled and protected by the same government, and by the same laws? When they enjoy the same rights, and have the same duties to fulfil? Yes, France is our country; all Frenchmen are our brethren, and this glorious title, by raising us our own esteem, becomes a sure pledge that we shall never cease to be worthy of it.

The line of conduct prescribed towards Frenchmen not of our religion, is the same as that prescribed between Jews themselves; we admit of no differences but that of worshipping the Supreme Being, every one in his own way.

> The love of the country is in the heart of
> Jews a sentiment so natural, so powerful, and
> so consonant to their religious opinions.

The Jews eventually won not only their legal emancipation but achieved integration. Napoleon repealed laws that discriminated against Jews but imposed new restrictions of his own, insisting they were needed to facilitate integration. "Our aim is to reconcile the belief of the Jews with the duties of the French, and to make them useful citizens, since we are resolved to remedy the ill in which many of them participate to the detriment of our subjects,"[11] Napoleon wrote to his Interior Minister Champagny.

Old prejudices die hard. By the time of the Dreyfus Affair, nearly ninety years later, a decorated, nationalistic French officer could still be subjected to the most profane ignominy and reminded that he is still an untrustworthy, traitorous Jew.

The dual loyalty accusation arose in most devastating fashion during the final years of Stalin's reign over the Soviet Union. Antisemitism in those lands survived the fall of the tsars and the Bolshevik Revolution. It was too deeply ingrained a phenomenon to simply disappear. Stalin's characteristic paranoia often found an outlet in antisemitism. His purges heavily targeted Jewish political rivals. He quietly introduced quotas on Jews in leading universities, cleansed the foreign service

---

11   Irène Delage and Emmanuelle Papot, "Napoleon I and the Integration of the Jews in France: Some Points of Interest," History Website of the Fondation Napoleon, https://www.napoleon.org/en/history-of-the-two-empires/articles/napoleon-and-the-jews/.

of Jews almost entirely, and ensured that the number of Jews holding party positions was severely limited.

To Stalin, the Jews were a people he could not quite place and could not quite understand. Were they ordinary Soviet subjects who had once held to a distinct monotheistic creed or were they a separate nationality to be broken and assimilated? Stalin vacillated but tended to favor the latter view, noting their distinctness with scorn and displeasure. "You can't go into a fight with them and you can't have a feast with them!"[12] Simon Sebag Montefiore observed that the Jews "irritated and confounded" Stalin. "Too much of a race for Hitler, they were not enough of a nation for Stalin."[13] Amongst the litany of complaints Hitler had with the Jews, he considered German Jews to be disloyal to the state and accused them of sabotaging Germany's campaign in World War I.

The Jews proved a reliable scapegoat for Stalin as well. They were disliked by the populace, easily shaped into whatever twisted phantasm suited the times and the agenda, and their "rootlessness" made it easy to cast them as serving foreign masters.

Stalin became increasingly obsessed with the question of Jewish loyalty. The Soviet people had suffered immeasurably through the war, but the German invasion of the Soviet Union had also seen special killing squads deployed for the purpose of identifying and annihilating Soviet Jewry. This resulted in the

---

12 Simon Sebag Montefiore, *Young Stalin* (London: Weidenfeld & Nicolson, 2007), 135.

13 Ibid., 294.

massacre of over 1.5 million Jews in the Soviet republics, largely through open-air shootings carried out with local collaboration.

In response to any perceived Jewish communal feeling that the genocide might engender, Stalin unleashed a wave of post-war anti-Jewish repression, seeking to erase any sense of Jewish distinctiveness which could turn into disloyalty just as the Cold War was descending.

1948–49 saw the closure of every Jewish cultural institution. On January 12, 1949, on Stalin's orders, the poet and actor Solomon Mikhoels was gruesomely murdered by Stalin's goons, poisoned, beaten, shot, his corpse thrown in the snowy streets and run over by a truck to mask the execution of the famous and revered performer. This was followed in 1952 by the Night of Murdered Poets, the execution of Jewish artists as traitors and spies on plainly ludicrous grounds. These charges included "staging plays in the theatre that glorified Jewish antiquity, shtetl traditions and life and the tragic doom of Jews, which aroused nationalistic feelings in Jewish spectators."[14]

The height of Stalin's febrile delusions about Jewish disloyalty saw the arrest of Jewish doctors who were tortured for being "murderers in white aprons," supposedly plotting to poison party officials at the behest of an "international Jewish bourgeois nationalist organization."[15]

---

14   Chaim Ben Yaakov, "80th anniversary of JAC: 'Dual loyalty' and the persecution of Soviet Jews," *Jerusalem Post*, August 15, 2021, https://m.jpost.com/diaspora/antisemitism/80th-anniversary-of-jac-dual-loyalty-and-the-persecution-of-soviet-jews-676681/amp.

15   William Korey, "The Origins and Development of Soviet Anti-Semitism: An Analysis," *Slavic Review* 31, no. 1 (1972): 111–135.

Stalin was unique for the scale of his crimes, but he was not alone in turning on the Jews under strain of war.

In a recorded phone call with his Secretary of State Henry Kissinger, President Richard M. Nixon thundered a classic exposition of the dual loyalties myth: "it's about goddamn time that the Jew in America realizes he's an American first and a Jew second."[16] The President also called the Jews "born spies."[17]

Writing in *The New York Times*, veteran US diplomat Dennis Ross revealed the suspicion still levelled at Jews working in the Pentagon:

> When I began working in the Pentagon during President Jimmy Carter's administration, there was an unspoken but unmistakable assumption: If you were Jewish, you could not work on the Middle East because you would be biased.
>
> However, if you knew about the Middle East because you came from a missionary family or from the oil industry, you were an expert. Never mind that having such a background might shape a particular view of the region, the United States' interests in it, or Israel. People with these backgrounds were perceived to be

---

16 Elspeth Reeve, "Some Newly Uncovered Nixon Comments on the Subjects of Jews and Black People," *The Atlantic*, August 22, 2013, https://www.theatlantic.com/politics/archive/2013/08/some-new-comments-richard-nixon-subject-jews-and-blacks/311870/.

17 Recording Date: July 5, 1971, Participants: Richard Nixon, Bob Haldeman, Ron Ziegler, Conversation Number: 537–004, https://millercenter.org/the-presidency/educational-resources/nixon-the-jews-are-born-spies.

> unbiased, while Jews could not be objective
> and would be partial to Israel to the exclusion
> of American interests.[18]

Ross also revealed how a routine background check for an appointee to a position with no connection to the Middle East again raised suspicions of Jewish dual loyalties.

> At one point, the investigator asked me a
> question that is routine in these background
> checks: Was this person loyal to the United
> States? I answered yes, without a doubt. But
> his follow-up question was if this person had
> to choose between America's interests and
> Israel's, whose interests would he put first?
> There was nothing subtle about this presump-
> tion of dual loyalty.
>
> "Why would you ask that question?" I asked,
> even though I realized I might not be help-
> ing the person using me as a reference. He
> answered, "Because he is Jewish." So I went on:
> "If he was Irish and had to work on problems
> related to Ireland or if he was Italian and had to
> work on Italy, would you ask that question?"[19]

---

18 Dennis B. Ross, "Memories of an Anti-Semitic State Department," *New York Times*, September 26, 2017, https://www.nytimes.com/2017/09/26/opinion/contributors/valerie-plame-antisemitic-state-department.html.

19 Ibid.

Speaking at an event in Washington in March 2019, Congresswoman Ilhan Omar said, "I want to talk about the political influence in this country that says that it is OK for people to push for allegiance to a foreign country."[20] Omar's remarks were directed at US supporters of the alliance with Israel and insinuated that those favoring such ties were acting out of "allegiance" to Israel rather than the United States. Omar was condemned from within her own party for using "antisemitic tropes that accuse Jews of dual loyalty,"[21] and perpetuating "the myth of dual loyalty, including allegations that Jews should be suspected of being disloyal neighbours or citizens."[22]

Jewish advocates and communal representative bodies that are supportive of Israel are routinely dismissed as being "lobbyists," implying they are agents for a foreign power and not citizens expressing their sincerely held views. In contrast, advocates for the Palestinian cause are rarely characterized as lobbyists.

As Manfred Gerstenfeld notes, the myth of Jewish dual loyalties "allows one to say, 'you are not really one of us.' In its most extreme form, the charge of dual loyalty amounts to an accusation of treason."[23] Like so many anti-Jewish myths it is

---

20 Clare Foran and Ashley Killough, "House Democrats to Update Resolution Condemning Anti-Semitism to Also Condemn Anti-Muslim Bias," CNN, March 5, 2019, https://edition.cnn.com/2019/03/05/politics/house-resolution-ilhan-omar/.

21 Ibid.

22 Gregory J. Wallance, "Ilhan Omar's Dual Loyalty Charge was about More than Anti-Semitism," March 7, 2019, https://thehill.com/opinion/campaign/432981-ilhan-omars-dual-loyalty-charge-was-about-more-than-anti-semitism?rl=1.

23 Chaim Ben Yaakov, "80th Anniversary of JAC: 'Dual loyalty' and the Persecution of Soviet Jews," *Jerusalem Post*, August 15, 2021,

self-fulfilling. Merely by posing the question of where a Jew's loyalties truly lie, their accusers cast suspicion on the Jews, which makes them feel estranged from the society they previously held to be their own.

Obedience to the laws of the land, a commitment to good citizenry and passionate civil participation are Jewish traditions that can be traced to the original exile of the Jews. The Prophet Jeremiah wrote from Jerusalem to the Jewish leaders in Babylon, counselling them to "seek the welfare of the city where I have sent you into exile, and pray to the Lord on its behalf, for in its welfare you will find your welfare." Jeremiah's decree was, and remains, the essence of good citizenry. Jeremiah further urged the Jewish community in Babylon "to multiply there, not decrease," and to "build houses and settle down… and to plant gardens and eat their produce."[24] In other words, the Jews were commanded to integrate fully and see themselves as a part of their new society. Wherever the Jews were afforded the opportunity to integrate, to contribute to the welfare of their cities and countries, they duly sought to do so.

In the responses of the Jewish Notables to Napoleon, it was pointed out that the Jews fought and died for their country, despite suffering cruel antisemitism by their own countrymen. "Many of them are covered with honourable wounds, and others have obtained, in the field of honour, the noble rewards of bravery,"[25] the Notables told the emperor. In the

---

https://m.jpost.com/diaspora/antisemitism/80th-anniversary-of-jac-dual-loyalty-and-the-persecution-of-soviet-jews-676681/amp.

24 Book of Jeremiah 29:6.

25 The Assembly of Jewish Notables, Answers to Napoleon.

Soviet Union, Jewish draft evasion was so widely assumed it became accepted fact. Yet 500,000 Soviet Jews fought in the Red Army during World War II.[26] Their heroism was heightened by the knowledge that should they be captured by the Germans their fate would be vastly different to that of their non-Jewish counterparts. Some 40 percent never came home. 550,000 Jews served in the US Armed Forces during World War II.[27]

The dual loyalty accusation remains a shrewd device of the antisemite. Often casually insinuated, it serves to entrench the view of the Jew as an "other," making them a permanent focus of suspicion, often barring their professional paths or undermining their right and freedom to publicly advocate for causes that are dear to them. In times of heightened anxiety or in the hands of a skilled leader, the myth can be used to turn a population against its own citizens and justify any manner of retribution or pre-emptive measure against the traitor in their midst.

26 Daniel Estrin, "The Forgotten Jews of the Red Army," *Times of Israel*, May 9, 2013, https://www.timesofisrael.com/the-forgotten-jews-of-the-red-army/.

27 "Jewish Americans in World War II," The National World War II Museum, New Orleans, https://www.nationalww2museum.org/war/topics/jewish-americans-world-war-ii.

MYTH 7

Oppressed to Oppressors

The cartoonist compares the situation of Palestinians in the Gaza Strip to that of Jews being shot by Einsatzgruppen, Carlos Latuff. Copyrighted free use, via Wikimedia Commons

"Israel has committed 50 massacres . . .
50 massacres, 50 Holocausts."
– Mahmoud Abbas.[1]

In May 2010, the words "Free Gaza and Palestine" were graf-fitied on a wall of the Warsaw Ghetto. The perpetrators had deliberately chosen the site to draw a connection between the events that transpired there and the situation of the Palestinians.

It bears noting what had occurred at the site of the defaced wall. The ghetto was established by the Germans in October 1940. Warsaw was at that time home to Europe's largest Jewish community, numbering around four hundred thousand. When the ghetto was established, the Jews of Warsaw and its environs were forced to relocate within the ghetto walls, an area of 1.3 square miles. Once the ghetto was sealed, malnutrition, disease and extreme hunger rapidly set in. Intestinal typhus and tuberculosis were rampant. The death rate rose to five thousand per month. A physician recorded that in March 1942, "the first case of hunger cannibalism was recorded. In a Jewish family the man and his three children died within a few days. From the flesh of the child who died last—a twelve-year-old boy—the mother ate a piece. To be sure, this could not save her either, and she herself died two

---

1   Hadas Gold and Nadeen Ebrahim, "Outrage over Palestinian Leader's '50 Holocausts' Remark," CNN, August 17, 2022, https://edition.cnn.com/2022/08/17/middleeast/abbas-holocaust-comments-berlin-mime-intl/index.html

days later."[2] The physician observed that the suffering and deprivation was so acute, "people fall asleep in bed or on the street and are dead in the morning. They die during physical effort, such as searching for food, and sometimes even with a piece of bread in their hands."[3]

Between June and September 1942, the surviving Jews of the ghetto were deported to the Treblinka death camp, where virtually all were killed by poison gas. The last batch of prisoners awaiting deportation raised a heroic, doomed uprising in January 1943 using small arms smuggled into the ghetto. They held out for nearly a month before the final resistors were either shot or transferred to the death camps.

The graffiti was by any measure a desecration of a mass gravesite and symbol of the Holocaust. But in a more incisive way, it constituted an act of replacement. The assailants could have expressed their solidarity with Palestinians anywhere, yet they chose a site in which Jews were forcibly confined, brutalized and eventually murdered, in a statement that the suffering of the Jews in that place has now been displaced by the Palestinians. The act was intended to convey that the Palestinians are latter day Jews, and their adversaries are latter day Nazis. In other words, the oppressed have become the oppressors.

The point was made even more explicitly by Catherine Nay, a news anchor who, in referring to a Palestinian boy killed in the crossfire between Israeli soldiers and Palestinian militants,

---

2   Raul Hilberg, *The Destruction of the European Jews* (New York: Holmes & Meier, 1985), 95.

3   Ibid.

said that the image of the cowering boy, "cancels, erases that of the Jewish child, his hands in the air before the SS in the Warsaw Ghetto."[4] The photograph to which Nay refers is of a Jewish boy of no more than ten, standing at the head of a line of women and children captured during the ghetto uprising, being led to their deportation, most likely to either the Treblinka or Majdanek death camps. Also in the frame is an SS officer, Josef Blosche, who indolently aims his submachine gun towards the boy's back.

The historian Lucjan Dobroszycki, who studied the photograph in an attempt to identify the boy, referred to it as "this great photograph of the most dramatic event of the Holocaust." Dobroszycki continued, "it requires a greater level of responsibility from historians than almost any other. It is too holy to let people do with it what they want."[5]

Yet to Nay, the photograph was now "erased." It was as if she could not simultaneously hold the two images, one of Jewish suffering and the other, to her mind, of Jewish-Israeli brutality. The earlier image made way, the Jews had surrendered their claim to sympathy and were now themselves perpetrators.

There are numerous explanations for such acts of erasure of Jewish suffering. The State of Israel was founded, at least in part, to serve as a place of refuge for the Jewish people. Sympathy and support for Israel has often been expressed

---

4   Catherine Nay, Europe1 network news anchor, cited in Ivan Rioufol, "Les médias, pouvoir intouchable?," *Le Figaro*, June 13, 2008.

5   David Margolick, "Rockland Physician Thinks He is the Boy in Holocaust Photo Taken in Warsaw," *New York Times*, May 28, 1982, https://www.nytimes.com/1982/05/28/nyregion/rockland-physician-thinks-he-is-the-boy-in-holocaust-photo-taken-in-warsaw.html.

through the prism of the Holocaust, which is taken to prove Jewish vulnerability and the need for a Jewish nation-state capable of ingathering threatened Jews rather than again leaving the protection of Jewish life to the international community. The necessity of such a place of refuge had been asserted long before the Holocaust, but the matter became self-evident with the wholesale destruction of the Jews and the failure of states and international bodies to prevent the genocide. If that history of persecution and suffering is "cancelled" or "erased," the case for a Jewish state is severely undermined. Thus, this technique can be usefully deployed as a rhetorical device in the Palestinian-Israeli conflict.

A further explanation can be gleaned for polling data on attitudes towards the Holocaust. Polling of antisemitic attitudes has consistently detected that large numbers of people resent Holocaust commemoration and education. Over 40 percent of Germans polled in 2019 felt that Jews "still talk too much about the Holocaust."[6] Replacing or erasing Jewish suffering is an effective way to avoid confronting both historical and contemporary antisemitism and offloading the guilt one might feel as a perpetrator or bystander or their descendant. If Jews are themselves perpetrators of genocide and similar crimes, why should we commemorate their suffering?

A particularly vicious example of this process of inversion, the recasting of Jews as perpetrators of Nazism rather than

---

6   Rebecca Staudenmaier, "One in Four Germans Hold Anti-Semitic Beliefs, Study Finds," *Deutsche Welle*, October 24, 2019, https://www. dw.com/en/one-in-four-germans-hold-anti-semitic-beliefs-study-finds/a-50958589.

its victims, took place on the sidelines of a United Nations conference in New York in 2009. The Nobel Laureate Elie Wiesel, who survived the Auschwitz and Buchenwald camps and the death marches, and lost his sister and parents in the camps, was surrounded by protestors and subjected to chants of "Zio-Nazi," including by a member of the official Iranian delegation.[7]

Aside from being a callous attack on an aged individual, the explicit equating of Zionism with Nazism is a pernicious form of revisionism, a dangerous rewriting of history. If Wiesel's support for Israel makes him a Nazi, then a Nazi is no longer a mass assassin of the most ruthless and sadistic kind. The term is devalued entirely making it impossible to understand the conduct and ideology it represents.

In April 2016, Ken Livingstone, a former mayor of London and senior figure in the British Labour Party, claimed that Hitler "was supporting Zionism before he went mad and ended up killing six million Jews."[8] Livingstone further claimed there had been "real collaboration" between the Nazis and the Zionists.[9] The historian Antony Beevor called Livingstone's remarks "grotesque." To be sure, Hitler at no point supported an independent Jewish state. The notion is

---

7   "Elie Wiesel Verbally Abused as "Zio-Nazi" by Ahmadinejad Entourage at Durban II," Simon Wiesenthal Center, April 21, 2009, https://youtu.be/zV3rw_QOD7U.

8   "Ken Livingstone to Quit Labour amid Anti-Semitism Row," BBC, May 21, 2018, https://www.bbc.com/news/uk-politics-44196298.

9   Rowena Mason, "Ken Livingstone Repeats Claim about Nazi-Zionist Collaboration," Guardian, March 20, 2017, https://www.theguardian.com/politics/2017/mar/30/ken-livingstone-repeats-claim-nazi-zionist-collaboration.

preposterous. His goal was Jewish destruction, not Jewish national liberation. Hitler said a Jewish state would be "nothing other than a center, in the form of a state, for the exercise of destructive influence by Jewish interests."[10] But Livingstone's ahistorical pronouncements received enormous coverage and served to form an association between Zionism and the supreme evil. Shortly after Livingstone made his comments, "Hitler Zionism" trended as a top google search in the UK.[11] Livingstone had simultaneously presented Israel as "Nazi-like," while shifting blame for the Holocaust, at least in part, to the Jews themselves.

This process of accusing the Jews of the very crimes to which they have been subject is not unique to pro-Palestinian activism. It has long been deployed by those who are incapable of coming to terms with persecution of the Jews and resent the empathy and understanding this history may arouse.

Rather than coming to grips with the suffering inflicted on the Jews in the name of the Church, Martin Luther blamed them for mass murder of Christians, calling them "thirsty bloodhounds and murderers of all Christendom." His call for the burning of synagogues and for Jews to be removed from their homes and encamped, a fate they would eventually

---

10 Ben Cohen, "The Mufti and the Holocaust, Revisited," *Jewish Chronicle*, October 28, 2015, https://jewishchronicle.timesofisrael.com/the-mufti-and-the-holocaust-revisited/.

11 "Ken Livingstone and 'Hitler Zionism,'" CST Blog, January 16, 2019, https://cst.org.uk/news/blog/2019/01/16/ken-livingstone-and-hitler-zionism.

suffer, was thus proffered as a defensive measure. "We are at fault in not slaying them," he declared.[12]

Similarly, while Hitler destroyed the nations of Europe and schemed global domination in the name of German *lebensraum* and a thousand-year Reich, Hitler blamed the stateless and scattered Jews for "plunging the nations once more into a world war."[13]

These audacious sleights of hand serve distinct functions in the spread of antisemitism. Firstly, they justify any act against the Jews as defensive measures. Secondly, they serve to arouse ever more hatred of the Jews for the double crime of falsely claiming persecution and persecuting others. Thirdly, they cleanse the consciences of the perpetrators, enabling them to commit unspeakable acts while maintaining a sense of morality.

This can occur through overt acts and deeds as exemplified by Hitler and Luther, or it can take more subtle turns.

Responding to a major piece by former Associated Press journalist Matti Friedman, who criticized the media's disproportionate focus on Israel, Friedman's former Bureau Chief both refuted the claims and sought to rationalize them. Steven Gutkin, who was AP's bureau chief in Israel from 2004 to 2010, explained that if there was any inordinate fascination with Israel and its perceived misdeeds it was because "the story of Israel is that of a nation rising from the ashes of the

---

12   Martha Sawyer Allen, "Lutherans to Apologize to Jews," *Tampa Bay Times*, October 16, 1993, https://www.tampabay.com/archive/1993/10/16/lutherans-to-apologize-to-jews/.

13   Jeffrey Herf, *The Jewish Enemy: Nazi Propaganda during the World War II and the Holocaust* (Cambridge, MA: Harvard University Press, 2008), p. 52.

worst genocide in human history, being attacked from all sides upon its inception, and depending on your point of view, ... it's also a story about the persecuted becoming the persecutors."[14] That a reputable media outlet would admit to covering the Israeli-Palestinian conflict subjectively through the lens of "the persecuted Jews becoming persecutors," simply because it could be made to fit within a quaint, satisfying formulation, is troubling indeed.

In January 2022, Rev. Dr J. Herbert Nelson II of the US Presbyterian Church invoked the oppressed to oppressors theme in accusing Israel of "slavery," which Nelson charged, ought to be "abolished immediately" given "the history of Jewish humble beginnings and persecution."[15]

In 1991, the Nation of Islam group, led by Louis Farrakhan, released an incendiary text titled *The Secret Relationship between Blacks and Jews*. The book aimed to show that "Jews have been conclusively linked to the greatest criminal endeavour ever undertaken against an entire race of people ... the black African Holocaust. ... The effects of this unspeakable tragedy are still being felt among the peoples of the world at this very hour."[16]

---

14 Stephanie Butnick, "Former AP Bureau Chief Responds to Article about Israel Coverage," Tablet Magazine, September 11, 2014, https://www.tabletmag.com/sections/news/articles/former-ap-bureau-chief-responds-to-article-about-israel-coverage.

15 Michael Starr, "Presbyterian Church Senior Official: Israel Commits 'slavery' against Palestinians," *Jerusalem Post*, January 21, 2022, https://www.jpost.com/christian-news/article-694190.

16 *The Secret Relationship between Blacks and Jews* (Nation of Islam book), 1991, quoted by Southern Poverty Law Center, https://www.splcenter.org/fighting-hate/extremist-files/group/nation-islam.

The book, widely panned by scholars of African American history for its dubious methods and its pre-determined findings, placed the Jews at the centre of the Atlantic slave trade which brought Africans as slaves to the United States.

A dispassionate review of the book and the scholarship on the slave trade by David Mills noted that the slave trade grew out of the sugar trade, as the colonial powers began cultivating sugar in the tropical climates of South America and the West Indies, an endeavor requiring enormous labor. Mills notes that while Dutch and Portuguese Jews were involved in the sugar business and therefore the slave trade in South America, they were small players, both due to their numbers and to the familiar restrictions on their ability to partake in lucrative and prestigious trades. As Eli Faber notes, the Jews were never a major player in any international trade in the Anglo-Saxon world except the diamond trade.[17] One British historian notes: "Most Jews in Barbados and Jamaica in the eighteenth century were small men, shopkeepers ... The sugar trade became increasingly concentrated in the hands of the sugar-planters' agents in London, a restricted and confined circle. [Jews] did not participate."[18] Mills concluded that non-Jews "controlled the slaving business in Colonial America."[19] Wim Klooster

17 Herbert S. Klein, "Review of *Jews, Slaves, and the Slave Trade: Setting the Record Straight,*" by E. Faber, *Journal of Social History* 33, no. 3 (2000): 743–745.

18 David Mills, "Half-Truths and History: The Debate over Jews and Slavery," *Washington Post*, October 17, 1993, https://www.washingtonpost.com/archive/opinions/1993/10/17/half-truths-and-history-the-debate-over-jews-and-slavery/6b2b2453-01da-4429-bd50-beff03741418/.

19 Ibid.

found that "in no period did Jews play a leading role as financiers, shipowners, or factors in the Transatlantic or Caribbean slave trades. They possessed far fewer slaves than non-Jews in every British territory in North America and the Caribbean. Even when Jews in a handful of places owned slaves in proportions slightly above their representation among a town's families, such cases do not come close to corroborating the assertions of *The Secret Relationship*."[20]

Yale academic David Brion Davis noted that the slave trade was conducted by all manner of ethnic and religious groups:

> The participants in the Atlantic slave system included Arabs, Berbers, scores of African ethnic groups, Italians, Portuguese, Spaniards, Dutch, Jews, Germans, Swedes, French, English, Danes, white Americans, Native Americans, and even thousands of New World blacks who had been emancipated or were descended from freed slaves but who then became slaveholding farmers or planters themselves.[21]

---

20 Wim Klooster, "Review of *Jews, Slaves, and the Slave Trade: Setting the Record Straight*," by E. Faber, *The William and Mary Quarterly* 57, no. 1 (2000): 217–219.

21 "AHA Council Issues Policy Resolution About Jews and the Slave Trade," American Historical Association, *Perspectives on History*, March 1, 1995, https://www.historians.org/publications-and-directories/perspectives-on-history/march-1995/aha-council-issues-policy-resolution-about-jews-and-the-slave-trade.

Additionally, Eli Faber concluded that the Jewish role in slavery was "exceedingly limited."[22]

To a great extent, the refutations and forensic deconstructions of *The Secret Relationship*, its abuse of statistics, its deliberate selectivity and its undenied attempt to "prove" that Jews were the orchestrators of Black misery, were irrelevant. As Mills noted, following publication of the book, "a small storm has been swirling—in the media, in academia, but mostly in the frictional world of ethnocentric politics—around the involvement of Jews in the African slave trade. It has been a tempest of hot rhetoric, factual confusion and moral recrimination."[23]

On the basis of the book, the controversial academic Lionel Jeffries could then blithely tell an audience, "Everyone knows rich Jews helped finance the slave trade."[24] Mills again: "Jeffries is clearly misusing historical facts to serve his animus against Jews today."[25]

The overwhelming weight of scholarship, essentially everything other than the Nation of Islam publication, points to a minor role for Jews in the Atlantic slave trade, one entirely consistent with their meagre numbers and their place in the societies of the colonial powers at the time. But as Herbert S. Klein observed in his review of Eli Faber's *Jews, Slaves, and the Slave Trade: Setting the Record Straight*, the Nation of Islam had succeeded in their aim of smearing the Jewish community, forcing them to answer ludicrous charges in the face of which

---

22 Eli Faber, *Jews, Slaves, and the Slave Trade: Setting the Record Straight* (New York: New York University Press, 1998), 143–146.

23 Mills, "Half-Truths and History: The Debate Over Jews and Slavery."

24 Ibid.

25 Ibid.

they could hardly remain silent. These denials fuelled further discussion, media coverage and press statements, all of which reinforced the association between Jews and slavery and created a false perception that the issue was at least controversial or contested.

"That it was necessary for a scholar to provide this much detail on this issue," wrote Klein, "tells us more about our own society than it does about the Jews and Africans in this period. Indeed one can understand much of the fascination with the Jewish role in the slave trade not as a matter of scholarly interest, but as part of an attack by anti-integrationist leaders on the Civil Right Movement and the 'rainbow' coalition."[26]

The Nation of Islam viewed the coalitions forming in the name of Black liberation and equality, of which Jews were a key part, as a step on the path to integration. This threatened the organization's vision of a society which maintained deeply entrenched racial boundaries, but with Blacks attaining the ascendancy and exacting their revenge. Farrakhan's predecessor, Elijah Muhammad, had warned, "Integration is against the desire and will of God who will restore the earth to its rightful owner (the Black Man)."[27]

The Jews had played a major role in the Civil Rights Movement, including by helping to fund and establish key civil rights groups including the National Association for the Advancement of Colored People (NAACP), the Leadership

---

26 Klein, "Review of *Jews, Slaves, and the Slave Trade: Setting the Record Straight.*"

27 Elijah Muhammad, "Our Saviour Has Arrived," 1974, quoted by Southern Poverty Law Center, https://www.splcenter.org/fighting-hate/extremist-files/group/nation-islam.

Conference on Civil and Human Rights, the Southern Christian Leadership Conference (SCLC) and the Student Nonviolent Coordinating Committee (SNCC). Between 1910 and 1940, Jewish philanthropy established some two thousand schools and colleges for the benefit of African Americans. And Jews made up half of the young people who participated in the Mississippi Freedom Summer in 1964.[28]

But there was a complexity to the relationship as well. As James Baldwin discussed in his crucial essay on Black-Jewish relations, "Negros are Antisemitic because They're Anti-White": growing up in Harlem meant having negligent landlords who were Jewish, pawnbrokers, shopkeepers, butchers who were also Jewish and who often treated them as badly as the white (and Black) police officers, teachers and shopkeepers that Baldwin encountered in his youth. Baldwin poignantly observes that the source of Black hostility towards the Jews "is not because he acts differently from other white men, but because he doesn't."[29]

While Baldwin sought to come to terms with this complex relationship, probing the historical and sociological sources of enmity in order to heal, others have merely set out to ignite it, and to turn Black against Jew, often to deadly effect.

---

28 "A Brief History of Jews and the Civil Rights Movement of the 1960s," Religious Action Center of Reform Judaism, https://rac.org/issues/civil-rights-voting-rights/brief-history-jews-and-civil-rights-movement-1960s.

29 James Baldwin, "Negroes Are Anti-Semitic because They're Anti-White," *New York Times*, April 9, 1967, https://archive.nytimes.com/www.nytimes.com/books/98/03/29/specials/baldwin-antisem.html?_r=1.

The Nation of Islam wickedly seized on tensions between the two communities and sought to transform them into open confrontation. "Who are the slumlords in the Black community? The so-called Jews. ... Who is it sucking our blood in the Black community?" the Nation of Islam declared.[30]

Around the time of the publication of *The Secret Relationship*, rioting broke out in the Brooklyn neighborhood of Crown Heights, where ultra-Orthodox Jews and the Black community lived in close, often stifling, proximity. Three days of violence were triggered when a car driven by an Orthodox Jew, trailing a motorcade of the spiritual leader of the Chabad movement, struck and killed a Black child and severely injured another. The ensuing violence saw the brutal murder of an Orthodox Jew from Australia, Yankel Rosenbaum, who was in New York researching for his PhD. The riots also saw looting of Jewish-owned businesses, hundreds of police officers and civilians injured and extensive property damage, in what Edward S. Shapiro called "one of the serious incidents of antisemitism in American history."[31] The New Republic called the riots an "antisemitic depravity." As noted in Edward S. Shapiro's analysis of the riots, "the rhetoric of the rioters was directed solely at Jews, they attacked only Jews, or those who looked like Jews, and the police who were protecting Jews."[32]

---

30 Speech by NOI national official Khalid Muhammad, November 29, 1993, quoted by Southern Poverty Law Center, https://www.splcenter.org/fighting-hate/extremist-files/group/nation-islam.

31 Edward S. Shapiro, "Interpretations of the Crown Heights Riot," *American Jewish History* 90, no. 2 (2002): 97–122.

32 Ibid., note 13.

The rioters had chanted, "Sieg Heil!," "Hitler was right" and "kill the Jew" as they made their way through the streets.[33]

While no single motive can explain why three days of racially targeted mass violence should be unleashed following a tragic road accident, the hatred inspired by demagogues and community leaders who blamed the Jews for the ills of Black society was a significant contributing factor.

Jews felt a historic responsibility to help uplift the oppressed African Americans, seeing in their plight a commonality of two peoples forged in slavery and held to be inferior through the ages. Meanwhile, African Americans "identified themselves as Old Israel suffering bondage under a new Pharoah."[34] James Baldwin observed that to devout Blacks, the identification with the Jews was so pronounced as to become a oneness:

> The Negro identifies himself almost wholly with the Jew. The more devout Negro considers that he *is* a Jew, in bondage to a hard taskmaster and waiting for a Moses to lead him out of Egypt. The hymns, the texts, and the most favored legends of the devout Negro are all Old Testament and therefore Jewish in origin: the flight from Egypt, the Hebrew children in the fiery furnace, the terrible jubilee song

---

33 Ibid., 112.

34 Judith W Kay, "The Exodus and Racism: Paradoxes for Jewish Liberation," *Journal of the Society of Christian Ethics* 28, no. 2 (2008): 23–50.

> of deliverance … The Covenant God made in the beginning with Abraham and which is to extend to his children and to his children's children forever is a covenant made with these latter-day exiles also: as Israel was chosen, so are they.[35]

The Nation of Islam sought to destroy this natural kinship by forcing Jews to defend baseless accusations that manipulated African American trauma.

The myth of Jewish domination of the slave trade was also used by a British Labour Party activist during the time of Jeremy Corbyn's antisemitism controversies, ostensibly to undermine sympathy for Israel, malign Corbyn's accusers in the Jewish community, and to decouple the historic ties between Britain's Jewish and Black communities. Echoing the language of the Nation of Islam publication, Jackie Walker spoke of "the African holocaust" and referred to Jews as "chief financiers of the sugar and slave trade."[36]

The Black Hebrew Israelite movement, a fringe group of hateful street preachers, have taken the "oppressed to oppressors" narrative to its preposterous conclusion. The Black Hebrew Israelites claim that it is they and not the Jews who were slaves in Egypt and that the Jews of today are in fact imposters who usurped their history. This strips modern Jews of their roots and identities as the descendants of slaves in Egypt and labels

---

35 Ibid., note 13.
36 "Labour Suspends Activist over Alleged Anti-Semitic Comments," BBC, May 5, 2016, https://www.bbc.com/news/uk-england-kent-36203911

the Jews as frauds and liars. This notion that the Jews usurped the identities of Blacks has experienced a disturbing prominence due to the remarks of Kanye West and Kyrie Irving beginning in October 2022. Both West and Irving have been widely condemned, but their posts have also garnered enormous amounts of discussion in which Jewish outrage and hurt have often been taken for evidence that West and Irving are truth-tellers wading into dangerous territory. West declared that his statements about the Jews were akin to standing, "in front of the tank in Tiananmen Square." The Nation of Islam praised West for "triggering a dangerous enemy."[37]

The emergence of Israel as an economic and military power, coupled with the achievement of peace between Israel and numerous Arab states, had led to a reframing of the Arab-Israeli conflict. No more seen as a clash of religions or a war waged by pan-Arabism, the belligerents are now seen to be powerful Israel and the stateless Palestinians. The rights and wrongs of the parties, the strength or weakness of their competing claims, are often made secondary to a more visceral urge to side with the party that appears more assertive and successful or the one that is seen as beleaguered and overmatched, depending on one's own preferences.

The accusations made by Israel's most trenchant critics that Israel practices unique forms of apartheid, genocide, ethnic cleansing and many other capital crimes in international affairs, skillfully plays to the "oppressed to oppressors"

---

37 Cited in "Unpacking Kanye West's Antisemitic Remarks," Anti-Defamation League, October 14, 2022, https://www.adl.org/resources/blog/unpacking-kanye-wests-antisemitic-remarks.

narrative, positioning the descendants of David as a Goliath and their adversaries as the noble Jewish king who courageously challenged and defeated him.

The "persecuted becoming persecutors" narrative is a modern-day Procrustean bed, so named for the sinister blacksmith of Greek mythology who cut or elongated the limbs of his victims to fit them perfectly into an iron bed. But no matter how one tries to hack apart the history of what happened to the Jewish people or to stretch the reality of contemporary events, it just doesn't fit. Still, the mutilations continue unabated—the activist intent on eroding support for the State of Israel, the charlatan hoping to incite ever more guilt-free antisemitic violence.

Such distortions place us all in renewed peril. For once history can be rewritten or revised, it becomes meaningless. It is not only the accounts of the past that become lost in this way, but the lessons derived from them. These lessons have never more relevant, never more needed than they are today.

Epilogue

In an essay published in *Harper's Magazine* in March 1898, Mark Twain wrote the following:

> The Jew has made a marvellous fight in this world, in all the ages; and has done it with his hands tied behind him. He could be vain of himself, and be excused for it. The Egyptian, the Babylonian, and the Persian rose, filled the planet with sound and splendor, then faded to dream-stuff and passed away; the Greek and the Roman followed, and made a vast noise, and they are gone; other peoples have sprung up and held their torch high for a time, but it burned out, and they sit in twilight now, or have vanished. The Jew saw them all, beat them all, and is now what he always was, exhibiting no decadence, no infirmities of age, no weakening of his parts, no slowing of his energies, no dulling of his alert and aggressive mind. All things are mortal but the Jew; all other forces pass, but he remains. What is the secret of his immortality?

Twain got some things wrong in his essay. He opposed the burgeoning Jewish independence movement that promised liberation or at least shelter from antisemitism, claiming "it would be politic to stop ... the concentration of the cunningest brains in the world" in a single country lest the Jews "find out their strength." He also nurtured the stereotype that Jews disloyally shirked their military service but retracted when presented with statistics that Jews served in the military in a larger percentage than their share of the population.

But he was right about the ability of the Jews to survive and outlive their tormentors. He was right to marvel at the scale of that achievement. That this numerically insignificant people who possessed no land for two thousand years, who did not retreat into anonymity but were at the very heart of world events, were subjected to all which this book records, and survived.

It is difficult to fully appreciate the challenges the Jews have faced in virtually every generation and in virtually every place. Yet for all the incentives to renounce their Jewishness or quietly let it lapse, for the brutal depletion of their numbers, there remains a people still bound by their belief in a single God, the God of Abraham, still adhering to the ethics and laws that first made them a people, still marking their ancient festivals, still reciting the Shema prayer, still binding their obligations on their hands and between their eyes through Tefillin, still inscribing them on the doorposts of their houses, and still living with a restless energy that fosters outsized contributions to civilization. Perhaps it is this success, the success of surviving and of stubbornly remaining who they always were, for which the Jews have never been forgiven.

It has become popular to argue that antisemitism is not the greatest threat to Jewish survival but in fact the key to it. That antisemitism has hardened the Jews, bettered them, endowed them with the fortitude and purpose to endure in a savage world. That without the hatred, that sense of mission is lost, and the Jews would assimilate and vanish. This view ignores the many positive virtues of being Jewish, the bonds of peoplehood, tradition, belonging, the refined wisdom of their customs, all of which make being Jewish profoundly rewarding, not because of being hated but in spite of it.

But it is true that antisemitism is an inescapable part of being Jewish. Surviving through the Inquisitions and pogroms and relentless vilification is defiance and strength. For many Jews, the "secret of their immortality," as Twain puts it, is an acute awareness of the extraordinariness of the Jewish story and a refusal to yield up something that is so rare and improbable. Would it not be a betrayal to surrender to indifference and apathy, to succumb to a shrug of the shoulders knowing what one's ancestors overcame to remain Jewish, to carry those stories and customs just a little further?

Primo Levi classified those who entered the nightmare of Auschwitz into the drowned and the saved. Those who were instantly pulled beneath the current by inhuman forces, never to be seen again. And those who somehow, through miraculous good fortune and some combination of necessary traits, positive and negative, were able to cling to life long enough to be saved. It is as though those Jews determined to remain Jews consider themselves living not only for their own limited sake, but out of the responsibility of being saved and out of a duty to the drowned.

This mindset gives life awe and purpose. It might also explain why, as Saul Bellow observed, the thing the Jew most fears is to be ordinary.

Antisemitism has indeed tied the hands of the Jews, as Twain wrote, but not of the Jews alone. Antisemitism ties the hands of all of us. To believe the myths contained in this book, to fear or hate or harm a person because of them is to suffer from defective reasoning, paranoia and a weak and wayward mind. This is not a condition that spawns creativity, beauty or human progress. Instead, it releases the darkest capacity of man, to burn, to torture, to destroy.

The Jews outlive their tormentors not as a coincidence or a quirk, but because in turning on the nation that gave the world its great religions and the ethics derived from them, they have turned on a vital part of themselves and, in doing so, have self-inflicted a mortal wound.

My hope for this book is that by exposing the squalor of anti-semitism, people will be less susceptible to it, less manipulated by it, and the tie that binds the hands of the Jewish people, and of all humanity, will be loosened.

Alex Ryvchin
Sydney, 2023

Essays and Speeches on Antisemitism by Alex Ryvchin

Why Did Everything Come So Easy to the Enemy?

The Ruthlessness of the Holocaust and the Dignity of Jewish Resistance[1]

———————

It is a great honor for me to speak on this day and to share my reflections on the theme of resistance during the Holocaust. Within this anguished phase of human history, we find the clearest displays of hatred, cowardice, heroism, and devotion ever observed and recorded. And so, here what is means to be human is revealed. And this is what makes the study and remembrance of the Holocaust essential.

The historian and former resistance fighter in the Vilna Ghetto, Meir Dvorzeki, demanded that, when we examine the question of resistance during the Holocaust, we do so only by seeking truth. "Do not depict the Jews of the ghettoes and the camps as better than they were," he said. "Do not engage in apologetics. But do not portray them as lesser than they were."

---

1 This is the transcription of the keynote speech for Holocaust Remembrance Day, given in Queensland, Australia, on April 16, 2023.

So let us consider this question of resistance.

The great Holocaust historian Raul Hilberg gives the most sobering, confronting assessment of how the Jews reacted to their immaculately choreographed extermination.

Hilberg explains that the 2,000 years of Jewish exile and dispersal, living in almost constant danger, had given rise to a precise, formulaic, and deeply internalized reaction to danger.

The Jews had come to believe that in order to survive they had to *refrain* from resistance. When faced with a persecutor, they would try to appease or placate them. They could try to ransom themselves. Make appeals to people in high places or to public opinion. Failing that, they accepted their fate. As the deluge would set in, they waited for it to pass over them and then subside.

They could not reason with the Crusaders or the Cossack horsemen, but they could outlast them, they collectively outlived them all. The Jews had come to believe that, because of the nature of God or man, they could not be annihilated. This too shall pass. *Am Yisrael Chai.*

They did not comprehend that Nazism was unique. Whereas Rome or Spain or Tsarist Russia were satisfied to exploit and brutalize or expel the Jews in their midst, Nazism would not rest until it hunted and destroyed every single living Jew.

As Hilberg concludes, the Jews could not make the switch. A two-thousand-year-old lesson could not be unlearned. And so, they were helpless.

The Germans, for their part, exhibited a chilling genius in their understanding of human nature, of how people can be broken so absolutely as to comply in their own destruction.

In the ghettos, the Germans appointed former Jewish communal leaders to form Jewish Councils with which they would liaise. This appealed to vanity and created the illusion that these Councils had some agency, some ability to impact what was unfolding.

They undoubtedly believed they were acting in the best interests of their people, doing all they could to obtain information, negotiate concessions, additional medical supplies, or hygeinic products, and maintain some semblance of routine for the condemned Jews by overseeing education, cultural performances, and support services.

We now know they should have been consumed with escape or rebellion and nothing else. Instead, they busied themselves educating children who would never become adults.

Armed resistance was strictly discouraged. It would only aggravate the Germans more and lead to even greater suffering. It seemed things could always get worse. Instead, these council leaders believed their powerful intellects could tame the beasts. They appealed to the Germans, wrote letters to them, each word carefully weighed by men of esteem, believing their fine rhetoric, wit, and logic must surely have some effect. In reality, they were helping to maintain the order and achieve the pacification of the enslaved people that made their extermination considerably easier.

The Nazis also extinguished the capacity for resistance among those they enslaved by employing every psychological device used by the captor and the torturer. They engaged in deception, assuring the Jews that deportation to death camps meant resettlement, gas chambers meant showers, and forced marches to predug graves meant reporting for work assignments. Jewish leaders were forever trying to find out from the Nazis what was going to happen next. The answers were always vague, dismissive, or dishonest. The truth that their annihilation was imminent was always kept from them.

They used the element of surprise, conducting pre-dawn raids of ghettos using baying dogs and live fire to shock the ghetto population into submission.

They degraded the Jews so completely as to crush any individualistic spirit. They used startling, unspeakable brutality to both shock and desensitize the Jews to suffering and they could even insert the occasional moment of respite, even a word of reassurance, to nurture docile compliance.

They kept the Jews off-balance at all times. Nothing stayed the same for very long. There were constant transports, new labour assignments to factories, movements from ghetto to camp, camp to camp.

Alexander Pechersky, a captured Jewish soldier of the Red Army, more on him later, spoke of this process as like the circles of hell in Dante's inferno. You constantly wondered what was next and when it would all end.

In this uncertainty, doing nothing seemed a better option than stepping out of line to face the sadism of the guards and an immediate and violent death. By the time death became an inescapable fact, it was much too late and the Jews usually fell into a paralysis and drifted to their graves.

In addition to all this, the speed and efficiency of the destruction process meant that the Jews had no time, no space, no means, and no physical capacity to resist in any meaningful or organized way.

We talk about the gradual process of destruction, beginning with the rise of Nazism and the Nuremberg laws and ending in the camps a decade later. But the actual mass killing process, still a quantum leap from the intense persecution preceding it, occurred not gradually but as a blitzkrieg.

In March 1942, almost eighty percent of the eventual victims of the Holocaust were still alive. Only twenty percent had by that point been murdered. By February 1943, just eleven months later, that number was reversed. Eighty percent of the six million were already dead. When the "final solution" became policy, murder became industrialized, and not a moment or a life was spared.

There were Jews who did manage to escape. Who somehow slipped away when being led to their killing field or made their getaway when being marched from their slave labor back to the camp. There was almost never a happy ending to their stories.

In the Lublin area of Poland, police battalions were given the task of combing the forests to find any last hiding Jews. The battalions called this the "Jew hunt." Squads of three or four would ride out eagerly each morning to discover the underground bunkers in which starving, petrified individuals or sometimes whole families hid, finishing them off with hand grenades or pistols, often subjecting them to torture first.

The only real choice the Jews had was complying in an anonymous death among the hundreds and thousands or hiding in the soil of a forest waiting for death to find you.

But acts of resistance great and small, organized and individual, can be found in every aspect and in every phase of the Holocaust.

Jews being deported to the camps, travelling in cattle cars for days with no food or water, would rip planks off the carriages with their bare hands, jumping from moving trains in the hope of making their escape.

In the Polish ghettos, clandestine publications were created and smuggled out beyond the ghetto walls to alert the outside world to the fate of the deported Jews.

Tens of thousands of Jews were saved by Jewish resistance organisations, which obtained false identity papers, established smuggling routes, and sheltered hiding Jews.

In Poland and the former Soviet republics, tens of thousands of Jews who managed to evade identification and capture participated in armed resistance. As many as 25,000 Jews fled the ghettos of western and central Poland to join partisan groups. Some 10,000 Jewish men and women from Lithuania did likewise.

A Jewish commando succeeded in blowing up a convoy bound for Auschwitz allowing 231 Jews to flee.

The most incredible instances of organised resistance occurred at the Sobibor Death Camp and at the Warsaw Ghetto.

Sobibor was a purpose-built extermination camp. Whereas at Auschwitz prisoners and new arrivals were selected for the gas chambers if they could not be worked do death, at Sobibor this process was reversed. Everyone was immediately gassed unless they were of the tiny minority selected for some form of work detail. As a result, almost no one survived Sobibor.

By October 1943, transports to the camp were becoming less frequent as there were so few Jews left to kill, and rumours began to circulate that the camp would soon be dismantled.

When the nearby Belzec death camp was dismantled, the last remaining prisoners were assured that, after they completed the work of exhuming and burning bodies and concealing the evidence of genocide, they would be transferred to a camp in Germany. Instead, they were sent to Sobibor to die.

One of the men from Belzec managed to sew a note into his clothing to the last inmates of Sobibor, which was discovered by a prisoner assigned to sort the clothing of Jews killed in the gas chambers.

The note said: "Be aware that you will be killed also! Avenge us!"

The uprising was instigated by a Polish Jew, Leon Felhendler. Felhendler knew the last prisoners in the camp were too broken to resist. But the arrival of Jewish Red Army prisoners of war gave Felhendler hope.

Among the new arrivals selected for work, he noticed a man named Alexander Pechersky.

When Pechersky saw a senior SS officer mercilessly beating a Jew who had collapsed while chopping wood, Pechersky leaned on his axe and stopped working himself. Intrigued by this defiance, the SS man proposed a challenge for his own sadistic pleasure. If Pechersky could split a tree stump in under five minutes, he would give him a pack of cigarettes. If he failed, he would be lashed twenty-five times.

Pechersky completed the task in four and a half minutes. To demonstrate he was a man of his word, the SS man offered up the cigarettes. Pechersky declined, saying that he didn't smoke. The SS man suggested some additional rations instead. The starving Pechersky replied that he found the standard camp provisions to be adequate.

Felhendler recognised in Pechersky a rare coolness and steel, and knew he was the only man who could lead the uprising.

When Pechersky heard a child's cry of "mama" coming from the gas chambers he realized that waiting it out was simply not an option.

Together, these men coordinated the simultaneous killings of several of the camp guards. They killed the acting commandant of the camp with an axe while the camp tailor was fitting him for a jacket that had belonged to a murdered Jew. The resistors then killed ten more SS guards before rushing the perimeter fence.

Only fifty-eight Jews of the 300,000 that were sent to Sobibor survived. The majority of those who participated in the uprising were either shot, blown up by land mines surrounding the camp, or mopped up by German patrols or Polish nationalists in the forests.

Felhendler survived but was murdered by Polish antisemites in his apartment in Lublin in 1945. Pechersky, the magnetic leader of the uprising survived in the forest, joined the partisans, returned to Soviet territory, survived Stalinism, and died in old age in the Soviet Union.

The Warsaw Ghetto Uprising, the eightieth anniversary of which we mark on this occasion, is one of the most significant events in Jewish history. And its lessons are critical to the future of our people.

In November 1940, the Germans established the Warsaw Ghetto, the largest ghetto in Europe. Around 450,000 Jews had been taken from Warsaw and its environs and crammed into an area of just over a square mile.

By April 1942, seventy-five percent of those Jews were dead. Most had been deported to Treblinka and gassed, others were shot in the ghetto or succumbed to disease and starvation.

A force of 700 Jews led by Zionist and Communist groups led the uprising. It unified Jewish nationalists and internationalists, hitherto bitter political foes.

They created a network of dugouts linked to the sewerage system. They smuggled in small arms, fashioned Molotov cocktails and took down collaborators, informers, and policemen inside the ghetto before engaging in combat with the SS.

They held the factories for as long as they could, jumping from collapsing buildings or escaping through the sewers when the SS battalions began the systematic destruction of the ghetto, scorching or toppling buildings and all inside them, to end the uprising.

For all their valor and determination, the Jewish fighters killed no more than sixteen of their tormentors. The uprising was crushed. The remaining Jews of the ghetto were either shot on site or deported to the death camps.

But the two-thousand-year-old pattern of helplessness in the face of torment that Raul Hilberg had observed had been forever broken.

Emanuel Ringelblum, who managed to escape the ghetto before being betrayed in hiding and executed along with the Polish family that hid him, wrote in lamentation:

"Why didn't we resist when they began to resettle 300,000 Jews from Warsaw to the camps? Why did we allow ourselves to be led like sheep to the slaughter? Why did everything come so easy to the enemy? Why didn't the hangmen suffer a single casualty? Why could 50 SS men and 200 Ukrainian guards carry out the operation so smoothly?"

No one among us can judge the actions of those placed in that purest rendering of hell that was the Holocaust. No one can say how they would have conducted themselves if faced with their circumstances.

I think the greatest difference between those who *could* resist and those who could not was their conception of hope. The resistors did not engage in self-delusion or false hope. They did not kid themselves that the killing process would just exhaust itself. Or that anyone was coming to liberate them. They knew they would die. Their hope was that by rebelling they could briefly create a new reality, a dawn they knew they would never see.

They resisted to restore their dignity and that of their people, to assert their honor, to restore some individualism, wrest back some scrap of freedom after everything good in this world had been burned and choked off. This, to me, is the height of bravery and nobility.

They also sought to inspire others and in this they succeeded. As Yehuda Bauer notes, "armed groups resisted the Nazis in 110 ghettoes and camps. There were 63 armed underground groups."

In addition to the uprising at Sobibor, Jews rose up in Treblinka and Birkenau. The Jewish resistance in Warsaw sparked major ghetto uprisings in Minsk and Bialystock.

In the dying words of the resistors, we see another common theme. Amidst it all was a crushing loneliness, a sense that they existed and were being erased as if on an island, unseen, unknown, cut off from all the world that was indifferent and oblivious to their tortured fate. That no one would know they ever lived and died.

But the resistors speak to us now. They tell us that they lived, did not succumb, they did not go quietly, they did not give up.

They teach us what it means to have courage, to be strong even when faced with an unstoppable force. To see a world and a destiny beyond our own lives.

And we, even here, so far in space and time from the scenes of the crimes, honor them, remember them, we speak their names, and we marvel at their greatness.

Thank you.

Jewish Pride Defies This Ancient Hatred[1]

For the most part, my childhood in Australia was free of anti-semitism. This led me to believe that we had left that hatred behind in the Soviet Union, when we emigrated in 1987. In Australia, my family moved house every couple of years as new migrants finding their way tend to do, and in my early teenage years we came to live in a modest, low-rise apartment block in middle class Randwick in Sydney's eastern suburbs. Soon we realized how deluded we had been. Directly above us lived a couple from Austria. The man was ageing but tall and vigorous, with a deep, resonant voice and a farmer's build. When he met my father, who spoke with a strong Russian accent and whose pale blue eyes and fair complexion hardly betray his ethnicity, the neighbor was genial to a fault. Then he saw my mother, and everything changed.

Upon learning that the new occupants were Jews, our neighbor would stand on his balcony and bellow at us, night after night, alternating between a thunderous guttural roar and a sneering tone full of menace, "Hitler didn't finish the job, I will finish it for him." An evening serenade that continued for weeks. It was terrifying to hear. It became difficult to sleep

---

1   This article originally appeared in the *Australian* on October 11, 2022.

beneath such a man, and it pained me to see the fear that returned full bore to my parents' eyes.

Why did he hate us so? What did he think we had done? What did he think we intended to do beyond living simple, honest lives as hopeful migrants in a new land? He surely would have had no coherent answer to these questions. He probably didn't ponder on them a great deal. But he knew with perfect certainty that the Jew, represented in that moment by my parents and their two boys, was something so loathsome, so repugnant, so unhuman, that he was justified in threatening repeatedly to kill a young family.

My youngest daughter will someday reflect on her first brush with antisemitism. It occurred on October 13, 2022 in Sydney's eastern suburbs when a large swastika was scrawled on the perimeter of her childcare center. The owners are Jewish as are most of the families there. Of course, the symbol meant nothing to my two-year-old daughter. But she may have detected things were different that day. The comings and goings. The tension of the owners. The anxiety of the parents wondering whether this was the act of another bellicose neighbour or of an idiot kid inspired by an idiot rapper. But perhaps it was a portent, the latest in an accumulation of incidents, street abuse, white supremacist flyers in mailboxes, suspicious characters lurking outside synagogues, that pointed to people in our communities who wished to do us harm. People afflicted by that ancient, consumptive hatred we know as antisemitism.

Antisemitism is an extraordinary condition, a pronounced defect in human reasoning turned outward. Unique among hatreds in very many ways. It has a tenacity and durability that sees it latch on to whatever the Jews hold dear and however they choose to identify themselves. For one antisemite, it is our original monotheistic faith that is so abhorrent. For another, it is our designation as a people, community, even a race. For others still, our nation-state is the embodiment of evil, the impediment to a better world. Each target is attacked with equal ferocity because in each case the target is the Jew. Yet it is not the flesh and blood Jew that is so hated. Rather, the mythical Jew, the beast the antisemite conjures just to have something to slay. The scheming Jew, the conspiring Jew, the all-powerful Jew, the vengeful Jew, the bloodthirsty Jew, the superior Jew, the inferior Jew, the capitalist Jew, the communist Jew, the moneyed Jew, the filthy Jew.

Even our identity, our right to be called a "Jew," is attacked. Kanye West calls us imposters who stole the identities of the "real" Jews, African-Americans, in a mangled libel invented by half-deranged street preachers in New York and globalized by the man who brings *Stronger* and *No Church in the Wild* to my workout playlist.

When Jews speak out against the hatred directed at us, we are accusing of "crying" antisemitism or "inventing" it. When we seek to define it so that others may understand a hatred that has brought unspeakable ruin to humanity, we are accused of acting with sinister motives, scheming to muzzle criticism of Israel rather than trying to protect our families.

My daughter's experiences with antisemitism have commenced a little earlier than I would have expected. As she comes of age, she will sense its lurking presence, she will learn of its savagery that caused her forebears all manner of unnatural death. But she will learn too that we are not victims, we don't seek or need pity, we don't plead with our oppressors, we outlive them; and we have learned through our agonies and our survival how to stand proud as a Jew and to strike back against those who do us harm.

Find the Pride and Duty in Our Survival[1]

It is an immense pleasure to be with you this morning. I always love coming to this school. It is the jewel of our community and a place that will equip you with the knowledge you need to succeed in this world. And the greatest piece of knowledge is knowing who you are and where you belong.

I'm referring to belonging to the Jewish people, something that is easy to take for granted, because we know nothing else. But I'm here today to pause my work and pause your studies to together contemplate what it means to belong to the Jewish people.

Firstly, you are all a statistical anomaly. As a Jew, you are part of a group of Australians that make up 0.38% of the total population. 99.62% of Australians are not Jews.

As a Jew, you are part of a group that makes up 0.185% of the world's population. 99.815% of the world is not Jewish.

By all rational reckoning you have no right to be here. The fact that you are here means that you are the descendants of that tiny sliver of humanity that somehow survived slavery in Egypt, then survived Roman slaughter and expulsion, survived the Spanish Inquisition in which Jews were forcibly

---

1   This is the transcript of the speech to Jewish students delivered in Perth, Australia on August 9, 2022.

converted or burned alive in public squares, survived the Crusaders who slaughtered every Jew they encountered as they passed through towns in Europe en route to Jerusalem, survived the pogroms in which Cossacks and peasants were let loose on our communities with unspeakable savagery, and you are the descendants of those who survived the most devastating killing machine ever constructed, an entire regime that consumed half the world and hunted and murdered every Jewish man, woman, and child in purpose-built killing factories and in thousands of mass shooting sites across Europe.

And yet you're here.

I know only a fraction of how I got here, to this day, with my Jewishness intact.

I know I'm an Ashkenazi Jew on both my mother's and father's sides, which means that my ancestors were among those Jews who survived the Roman conquest of ancient Israel in the second century and were expelled after our people rose up in an attempt to overthrow the Emperor Hadrian and live freely in our own land.

They would have made their way to the heart of the Roman Empire, probably to France or Germany, where they settled in the Rhine Valley where dozens of Jewish communities were established.

In the eleventh century, the Crusades began, where ordinary Europeans were encouraged to take up arms and march to Jerusalem to capture the Holy City and prevent the spread of Islam. But the Crusaders were soon refocused by sinister leaders and clerics—why march all the way to Jerusalem to fight non-believers when Jews are living right under our noses.

In the carnage that ensued, the Jewish communities in the Rhine virtually vanished.

My ancestors must have either fled just before the Crusaders wrought their destruction or somehow survived, moving eastward in the hope of finding a peaceful existence in what is today's Poland, Russia, or Ukraine. They might have enjoyed a generation or so of peace under rulers who let Jews study, work, and pray in peace.

But as the Russian Empire was formed and began to expand, the Jews caught within it were subjected to cruel laws that regulated where we could live, where we could work, and where we could enter. As a result, my ancestors were reduced to an inferior status, living outside the protection of the law, living in constant fear of being set upon by a drunken mob.

My great-grandfather kept an axe by his front door his whole life, in readiness for the pogrom, the frenzied mob attack that wiped out entire Jewish communities in Russia and led to the birth of the Zionist movement to give us our own home, to find our rightful place in peace and security.

Then came the Russian Revolution, the royal family was overthrown and murdered, and in its place emerged a new tyranny, a new system of brutality, which relied on a secret police that shot anyone suspected of ideological deviation. A system of slave labor camps was created where anyone under the slightest suspicion could be sent to Siberia in horrendous conditions, from which many would never return.

My family survived all that. They survived the brutal Civil War that followed the Revolution. A famine in the Ukraine that killed as many as eight million people. Stalin's Great Terror. But somehow, none of this was the worst was to come.

On June 22, 1941, Nazi Germany invaded the Soviet Union with three million soldiers in the largest invasion in history. The entire Soviet nation suffered during that war in unimaginable ways. Millions starved as the Germans destroyed everything in their path or besieged cities for months at a time. Twenty-eight million Soviet citizens died during the war.

Men of all ages, including in my family, were called up to fight, often with no weapons, sent to run hopelessly at the most devastating fighting force ever assembled. Many of my distant relatives fell in battle defending a motherland that despised them.

But there was a special hell awaiting the Jews of the Soviet Union. You see, as the German army advanced deeper and deeper into Russian territory, just behind its front lines rode teams of elite soldiers, educated men in their thirties, including lawyers, doctors, scholars, chosen for a special assignment. Their mission was to ensure that, once the army had captured a town or a city, every single Jew living in it was to be murdered. These killing squads were known as *Einsatzgruppen*.

My family was living in the city of Kyiv at this time, a city many of you will now be familiar with as the capital of Ukraine. The German army encircled the city in September 1941 in what Hitler called the greatest battle in history. The last Soviet soldiers withdrew on September 19.

On the same day, the *Einsatzgruppen* entered the city. A few days later, signs were plastered throughout the city ordering the city's Jews to assemble by the gates of the Jewish cemetery with their documents, valuables, and winter clothing, at a horrible rocky expanse called Babyn Yar, which means "old woman's ravine." The signs warned that any Jew who didn't present there would be immediately shot.

The next morning, the Jews began to make their way by foot to the assembly point as their Ukrainian neighbors lined the streets to watch. Those who tried to hide were ratted out by their neighbors.

After two days, the Germans declared the city to be free of Jews. Babyn Yar today is no longer a valley. 100,000 victims buried within flattened it out.

Just before the city fell to the Germans, all civilians who were fit for work were evacuated to factories far from the fighting so that they could help build weapons, tanks, and planes for the Soviet army. My grandparents were among those to be evacuated. Had they stayed, they would have been shot in that ravine. I wouldn't be here today. My family's story would have been snuffed out like so many others.

My story is unremarkable. Every Jew from the Soviet Union has lived some variation of this story. If your family is from South Africa, your parents and grandparents can tell you their story, which is similar to mine except that, rather than settling in Ukraine, they settled in Lithuania. Thankfully, your families had the wisdom to recognize there was no future for them in Lithuania and they left for South Africa in the early 1900s. Had they stayed, they would have almost certainly perished—over ninety percent of Lithuanian Jews were exterminated. And their stories would have ended in forest pits and killing fields.

If your families are Sephardi and not Ashkenazi, they have their own stories to tell, mob violence, upheaval, fear and terror, survival, sorrow, beauty, and wonder all the same—just in a different setting.

My advice to you is, learn your stories. They are your birthright. They reveal much about why you are as you are. They are full of magic, of blind luck, of courage, of miracles. That's the only way you could have gotten here.

And take strength from your story, from belonging to a people that have contributed so much to humanity and have survived and endured where other ancient peoples, and the empires who oppressed us, have simply vanished.

Educate, Engage, Enforce: How to Fight Antisemitism[1]

There is a story that emerged from *Kristallnacht*, of the Jews of one German town being forced to line up and spit on a Torah taken from the ransacked synagogue. To the delight of the sneering Nazi thugs, even the most observant of the community did so, choosing debasement over death. When it came to the turn of a Jew named Slater, long lapsed and a known criminal, he responded, "I've done a lot of miserable things in my life, but this I won't do."

Slater showed us that the Jewish essence resides within each of us and, while it may lie dormant for considerable time, it can never be extinguished.

The antisemitism we face today is of an entirely different character and severity. But the hatred of our people can also slumber. When it rises, and it always does, it is with an almighty lash.

In statistics compiled by the Executive Council of Australian Jewry (ECAJ), we see a steady rise in incidents. We hear of horrific cases of antisemitic bullying and abuse in schools,

---

1   This article originally appeared in the *Australian Jewish News* on July 21, 2022.

a toxic campus environment, and regular instances of vilification and harassment.

We have seen the baiting of Jewish students through metres-high "f*ck Zionism" graffiti and a sequence of student council resolutions each seeking to outdo the other with how many slurs can be inserted into a single motion. The unmistakable aim of this is to silence Jews. To show them that their acceptance comes at the cost of relinquishing something sacred to virtually all Jews, an emotional or ideological connection to Israel. It forces them to spit upon an inseverable part of being Jewish.

As the writer and comedian John Safran recently noted, a Greens member of the South Australian parliament opposed the adoption of the International Holocaust Remembrance Alliance working definition of antisemitism, because "it is not clear what is a Semite . . . [which] includes a much broader range of people than the Jewish people." As Safran further noted, an article in the *Green Left Weekly* recently spoke of "anti-Arab antisemitism."

Both instances are a form of erasure, a tactic popular among despotic regimes and their enthusiasts, that seeks to obliterate the true meaning of words thus vaporizing the thing itself. The aim here is to place antisemitism beyond the grasp of understanding and therefore beyond counteraction.

The antisemitism of the left-Stalinist variety has always traded in euphemisms to maintain the façade of anti-racism and claim the moral high ground from political enemies. From the 1950s, "Jew" gave way to "Zionist," while classical themes and slanders were retained – the tentacled beast manipulating the media, governments, and finance; the lust for the blood of the innocents, the obstacle to a better, purer world.

They equate Jewish Israelis with those who slaughtered their kin in forest pits and death camps. They hold the very concept of a state for the Jews as a racist endeavour while having no complaint with the idea of the nation-state itself, of which Israel is but one of many. They shrug at French, German, or Polish policies to maintain a national character in a tumultuous world while decrying the presence of the *menorah* or Star of David on Israeli postage stamps as evidence of a diabolical regime ripe for toppling.

The denials and gaslighting deployed by these antisemites have made teaching an understanding of antisemitism even more urgent.

Education for its own sake is futile. We must educate through a combination of real-life encounters with Jews to demonstrate who we are as a people and a community; by imparting knowledge of antisemitism and the ruin it brings; and providing the tools to both understand and take action.

Napoleon said, "without education there is no present and no future." With this education, our future as Jews will be protected and the forces against us will be exposed for what they are.

How We
Avenge 9/11[1]

A few weeks before the surrender of Nazi Germany in May 1945, a group of survivors of the Holocaust met in Bucharest to mark Passover, the Jewish festival of freedom. Among the group was Abba Kovner, who had escaped the Vilna ghetto and led a partisan campaign that struck at the Nazis and their collaborators from the forests of Lithuania. Kovner was consumed with the desire for revenge. "He will repay them for their iniquity and wipe them out for their wickedness," he told his fellow survivors at that Passover gathering, invoking Psalm 94 and God's promise to deliver vengeance upon the enemies of Israel.

After the war, Kovner and his comrades, known as the "Avengers," hatched a series of plots to exact retribution for the murders of their families and the near annihilation of the European Jews. Most were aborted but the Avengers did succeed in getting their operatives into the kitchen of the Stalag 13 POW camp at Langwasser near Nuremberg, where Nazi SS, the units responsible for the implementation of the "final solution," were being held. They planned to poison the bread

---

1   This article originally appeared in the *Australian* on September 14, 2021.

of the prisoners, but the poison failed to take full effect and not a single SS man died.

The pursuit of revenge after the Holocaust proved futile. How does one even begin to avenge such a crime, really a sequence of millions of individual crimes, including the murders of one million children, carried out by hundreds of thousands of perpetrators across Europe?

It is a stale cliché to say that success is the best revenge, but it is true all the same. The real revenge that the Jewish remnants took against those who pursued their obliteration was their survival and the reestablishment of a successful national centre for the Jews in their ancient lands, which revived Jewish culture and enhanced Jewish scientific, cultural and scholarly contributions to the world. Abba Kovner would become one of that state's greatest poets.

For those of us who watched the carnage of 9/11, the desire for revenge was a difficult emotion to suppress. "Revenge is the first law of nature," wrote Napoleon as a young man. It was certainly just and necessary to find those who masterminded the murders of 2,996 people and to incapacitate terrorist organisations who would pursue further attacks. As the Babylonian Talmud teaches, "if someone comes planning to kill you, rise and kill them first." But the desire for revenge goes beyond justice or prevention. It aims to redeem those whose lives were taken and to restore their dignity. A noble aspiration but one that is more often than not unattainable and the pursuit of which can corrode the soul.

The true revenge for 9/11 ought to have come in the form of global unity comprised of people of all faiths and none, who stood in common revulsion at the medievalism of terrorism and shared a determination to drive fanaticism from our societies.

Instead, the 9/11 attacks did precisely what their mastermind had intended. Beyond killing thousands of innocent peoples, the attacks shook the self-confidence of the West. They divided us into doves and hawks, established fault lines that persist today and caused a collective questioning of our very ideals. Many would conclude that the pillars of our society, enlightenment, rationalism, human freedoms were actually void and corrupt as the Al-Qaeda assassins had charged from their caves.

9/11 also triggered a dangerous defect in our thinking. Instead of understanding that the terrorists were motivated by a barbarism and bloodlust of which mankind has always been capable, we began to believe that we had brought this upon ourselves. We assumed that rational objections to policy were governing the thoughts of those for whom slaughtering morning commuters and teenage girls at pop concerts constitutes success. But rationalism is not universal or innate. It occurs only in those who are raised in its traditions and teachings. And religious extremism does not breed rationalism, it crushes it.

This doomed path of inquiry produced a narrative that Israel's conflict with the Palestinians and US support for Israel was the root cause of radical Islam's desire to overthrow the West. The academics Walt and Mearsheimer claimed that US support for its democratic ally was a predominant source of anti-American terrorism and urged punitive measures against Israel. High school textbooks in Britain also suggested that Israel's creation was the root cause of Islamist terrorism and the motivation for 9/11.[2] Rather than confronting radical Islam's fanatical hatred of the Jews and Bin Laden's stated mission to "punish the oppressive Jews and their allies," such thinking in effect validated their racism and bowed to it.

The wicked sectarianism on display in Syria, Iraq, Yemen, and Lebanon finally made mockery of the view that, if only Israel withdrew from the West Bank, Al-Qaeda, ISIS, Jemaah Islamiyah, and the rest would promptly beat their swords into plowshares and their spears into pruning hooks.

As we all do, I still vividly recall September 11, 2001. I came into my torts law class after watching the second plane destroy the south tower. Our lecturer announced that class was cancelled. "I'm not going to lecture you about the 'reasonable person' test when such unreasonable people exist in the world," he said. Unreasonable people will continue to exist and inflict misery. But our revenge and our victory lie in the survival of free societies, our reasonable, rational thought, and our unified purpose to uphold precisely that which the terrorists sought to destroy.

---

2   Jeremy Sharon, "UK School Textbook Asks How Creation of Israel Was Cause of 9/11 Attacks," *Jerusalem Post*, February 20, 2020.

Have We Not Avenged?

The Destruction of the Soviet Jews and Revenge through Remembrance[1]

Thank you very much. It is a tremendous honour and a privilege to follow in the footsteps of some very fine Australians in delivering the keynote at the most important annual event for our Sydney Jewish community.

I wish to acknowledge the community leaders present including the president of the ECAJ Jillian Segal AO, rabbis, members of the federal and state parliaments and members of the diplomatic corps with us this evening.

And finally, but foremost, I wish to acknowledge the survivors of the Holocaust, the most esteemed and treasured members of our community, those who emerged from the greatest crime in history and enlighten our society with their dignity and strength.

What happened to the Jews in the Soviet Union during World War II remains one of the least understood aspects of the history of the Holocaust. The crimes committed there

---

1   This is the transcription of the keynote speech for Holocaust Remembrance Day, given in Sydney, Australia, on April 8, 2021.

were too vast, too swift, too brutal, too complete. They left few survivors to tell the story. They left no large camps or crematoria, edifices of human monstrosity to educate and remind. The very few who survived the crimes, the very many who committed them, and the Soviet authorities who could not prevent them, were all satisfied to obliterate them from consciousness. All across the once unknowable lands of the former Soviet Union are killing fields, thousands of sites, most of them unmarked, many disturbed and desecrated by construction, in city parks and forests and gentle valleys where the entire communities of murdered Jews lie beneath.

The extermination of the Soviet Jews took place under the cover of the German invasion of the Soviet Union that commenced on June 22, 1941. Stalin was caught completely unprepared, having long dismissed Churchill's warnings of ominous German troop movements and intelligence reports of a looming attack as mere British agitation and warmongering. The Stalinist killings of the nation's finest generals during the purges of the 1930s and the enslavement of millions of citizens in Siberian gulags, had left the mighty Red Army a pitiful husk, utterly incapable of containing the rapid advance of the regular German forces, the *Wehrmacht*.

The invasion was the largest military operation in history, involving more than 3.8 million German and Axis troops. Within three weeks of its commencement, the Soviet Union had lost two million men and seen the destruction of a significant portion of its officer corps. Within a month, the Germans had captured territory twice the size of France.

But this was an altogether different kind of war, one unprecedented in human history. Here the primary aim was not strategic victory or territorial acquisition, but the total destruction of what Hitler termed Judeo-Bolshevik influence. Hitler declared this would be "a battle of annihilation." *Rassenkampf*, race war.

In the months leading up to the invasion, the German high command had to solve the problem of how to simultaneously conduct a conventional military campaign on an enormous scale that relied on maximum force delivered with lightning speed, while diverting resources for the hunt of a civilian population, well integrated and spread throughout towns and cities and villages across thousands of miles of Soviet territory.

By March 1941, it was agreed that special task forces would be formed for the implementation of "collective measures" against the Jews. These task forces would receive supplies and quarters from the army, but would pursue their own mission taking their orders from the Chief of the Security Police Reinhard Heydrich.

As the German army rapidly swallowed ground, bringing millions of Soviet citizens under their control, these special units, moved fast on the heels of the regular army, sometimes even appearing on the front lines to trap the Jews before they could discover their fate. Elite, mobile and merciless, these special units, mobile killing squads, were known as *Einsatzgruppen*.

The entire Einsatzgruppen consisted of only around 3,000 men divided into four, Einsatgruppe A, B, C, and D. Each travelled with a different army group of the advancing German force meaning they could fan out and cover enormous territory from Odessa on the Black Sea in the south to Riga and Tallin on the Baltic in the north.

Their strength came from their mobility, their freedom to peel off from the regular army to enter towns and villages to begin their hunt. After striking at a location, the killing squads would return to conduct further sweeps, sometimes only hours after the first, other times weeks would pass, but they would always return to ensnare any Jews who had avoided the initial dragnet.

The precise methods of killing varied. In Dalnik, outside Odesa, the Jews were crammed into warehouses and machine-gunned through holes in the walls and then set alight. In Zmiyevskaya Balka in Rostov, the men were marched to a ravine outside the city and shot to death while the Jewish women, children and elderly were gassed in trucks before being deposited in the ravine. Jews were shot in forest pits they were forced to dig, in anti-tank trenches in which they were forced to lie, row upon row upon row, the living lying atop the wounded and dead, awaiting the bullets from above. Sometimes they were simply buried alive to save bullets. The locals would report strange movements of the earth and wails from within for days after the massacres.

Other times locals were incited to simply club Jews to death. In Bogdanovka, 5,000 sick and infirm Jews were placed in stables which were sprinkled with straw and set alight. 43,000 more were marched into the forest in groups of 300, forced to kneel naked in the ice, and shot.

The sheer speed of events, the lightning German advance, the emergence of the killing squads, left the Jews in a bewildered daze. In the span of, sometimes, a few hours, the Jews were plucked from their ordinary, peaceful lives, taken to killing sites, and executed despite having committed no crime.

The Germans often reported a strange calmness among the Jews as they drifted in a dream-like disbelief until the moment of death, their already meager capacity to resist overwhelming force entirely neutralized by the deathly efficiency of the killers.

In places like Riga, Vilnius, and Slonim, ghettos were formed so that skilled Jewish workers who had been spared in the initial massacres because of their utility could be used as slave laborers until non-Jewish workers could be trained to replace them. When it came time to liquidate a ghetto, small numbers of Jews were taken to dig mass graves outside the city in readiness for the slaughter. Now knowing what fate awaited them the next morning, a communal dread set in. The Jews in the ghetto made feeble, futile last appeals to the Germans. The killing operations would begin either at a dawn or sometimes in the middle of the night. First the ghetto would be encircled by police units. SS men and local collaborators would then enter with flashlights shouting for the Jews to open their doors. Those who submitted were assembled and led to the graves to be shot. Those who hid were burned alive or exploded with grenades.

The sheer volume of the killing was enormous. Each day, the Einsatzgruppen would dutifully report of 23,600 Jews liquidated in Kamianets-Podilskyi, 33,771 in Kyiv, 35,000 in Mykolaiv, and on it went, day after day.

But so small a force that had no knowledge of local communities or hiding places could not have killed on such a scale without help. In virtually every place they entered they were aided by locals who knew the Jews and knew the hiding places. In Lithuania, Estonia, and Ukraine they formed auxiliary police units that took part in every phase of the killing process, often carrying out the bloodiest work for spare the nerves of the Germans. Ordinary civilians also relished the opportunity to dispossess, brutalize, and destroy their Jewish neighbours. In Kaunas, a young Lithuanian man bludgeoned Jews to death with a crowbar before a crowd that cheered every killing. In Latvia, local university students assisted in the murder of Jews. In Proskuriv (now Khmelnytskyi), Ukraine, Ukrainians lined the streets and applauded as Jewish women were stripped and led to be shot. This was indicative of the reactions of local populations throughout the land, which aside from isolated cases of heroism, ranged from apathy to sadistic relish.

By the time the Germans were forced into retreat some 1.5 million Jews lay murdered across Soviet lands. Ninety percent of Lithuanian Jews were dead. In Latvia, only a few hundred Jews remained. Estonia had been declared completely free of Jews as early as 1942. 800,000 Jews from Belarus were dead. The storied black soil of the Ukraine bulged disfigured from more than 2,000 killing sites across its land. Babyn Yar, a block from my own family's home, was just one, the most famous killing site, but every city, every town, every village, witnessed its own Babyn Yar, its own killing field.

One of the reasons why the Soviet phase of the Holocaust has often been overlooked is that it shatters many of the prevailing theories and concepts to emerge from the study of the Holocaust. That there was a phased, discernible progression from Nuremberg to *Kristallnacht* to the adoption of the "final solution" in Wannsee in January 1942. That there was a gradual process of dehumanisation, of heinous words leading to heinous acts. That the insidious drip of cunning propaganda slowly turned populations against their Jews.

But the systematic annihilation of the Jews had been operating in the Soviet Territories for six months before Wannsee. Here, there was no careful process of classifying Jews, or expunging them from public life, confining them to ghettoes rife with disease until these people resembled the insular, wretched, diseased species that propaganda had depicted them to be, and local populations now ached for their removal. In the east, no such measures were necessary. Local populations had been primed into supporting anti-Jewish measures by governments, churches, and nationalist heroes over centuries of Cossack rebellions and pogroms. In the Soviet Union, in virtually all places the Einsatzgruppen entered, the Jews were simply summoned and shot with no outrage and no opposition.

Who were the assassins of children and old women on the eastern front? Who were the men that filled the ranks of the Einsatzgruppen, that rode down highways and dirt tracks on motorcycles and in cars, entering new towns and villages like merry adventurers to attend to the killing of 875 Jewish girls and women in Berdychiv or the shooting of 90 Jewish children in Bila Tserkva. These were not young soldiers trained to kill on command or criminals plucked from German jails and now let loose. Virtually all were educated men in their thirties and forties. One of the first Einsatzgruppen commanders held a doctorate in jurisprudence. Another officer was a physician. Many were lawyers. One was an opera singer. These were deep thinkers, cultured men who plainly saw the absurdity of shooting every single Jew as a Bolshevik agitator. They knew, yet they completed their work with a perfect efficiency, applied all their learning and talent to it, never wavering in their task.

Gone were entire communities, dynasties of scholars and artists, gone were the Jewish peasants tending the land, the pious, secluded families seeking wisdom in ancient texts, the middle-class merchants of the cities, the teachers, the drunks, the scholars, the poets, the vagrants, the bankers and the children. All of them. Executed as mortal threats to German survival and human progress. In the final wash it just didn't matter how absurd the idea of their collective guilt was.

The people believed this lunacy because they wanted to believe it. And if they were wrong and they had just extinguished millions of lives for no reason at all and their misfortunes would not go to the grave with the Jew, well at least they have blown off a little steam and enriched themselves in the process.

The thousands upon thousands of individual stories of horror, the scores of dispassionate historical texts, Hollywood films, novellas, and memoirs that depict these events all seek, and all fail to fully explain why human beings would act this way to their fellow man.

What discord existed in the hearts of ordinary men and women that they would shed their humanity entirely, and seize with unrelenting purpose the opportunity to dispossess, humiliate and destroy their neighbors simply because they were Jewish? This is the imponderable at the heart of the Holocaust.

There is a story told by the scholar and Nazi hunter Efraim Zuroff, at the beginning of one of his books. He writes about Shimon Dubnow, a brilliant writer of Jewish history who was among those Jews murdered in the Riga Ghetto. And as he was being taken out to be shot, he called out to the Jews around him. He said, "Yidn, farschreibt"—"Jews, write it all down, record everything." Meanwhile, in Kaunas, Lithuania, Jews wrenched from their homes and taken to die, also left a final message, which they had scrawled on the walls: "Yidn, nekoma"—"Jews, take revenge."

I think about these words often and I am compelled to write and speak about what happened to our people in part by Shimon Dubnow's injunction, even though this history is hard to read, hard to write and hard to speak.

But the revenge, a sentiment to which I am equally drawn, is more elusive. How can one avenge the most audacious, extensive, inhuman crime in human history? Really a sequence of millions upon millions of crimes rendered on the weak and defenceless when the opportunity arose, committed by hundreds of thousands of individual perpetrators who for the most part faced no justice or consequences at all.

But when I think about what those crimes sought to achieve, which is the complete termination of Jewish existence and the extinguishment of every last Jewish soul so that we and our children should never have been born, by living and living as Jews, by creating new Jewish life, have we not taken our revenge?

When the killers retreated, they sought to remove all trace and memory of their crimes, by hastily exhuming and burning bodies. Yet we know. And we come together to remember and to educate, we dedicate new museums, we erect new monuments to our sacred dead, even here in our great city, have we not avenged?

And we should go on avenging, daily, through our survival, our pride, and our strength. That will be our victory.

The Crisis of Zionism[1]

When the French playwright Edmond Fleg attended Herzl's
Third Zionist Congress in Basel in 1899, he marvelled at the
scene. "I looked about me. What Jewish contrasts! A pale-
faced Pole with high cheekbones, a German in spectacles,
a Russian looking like an angel, a bearded Persian, a clean-
shaven American, an Egyptian in a fez, and over there, that
black phantom, towering up in his immense caftan, with his
fur cap and pale curls falling from his temples." Fleg saw the
sum of Jewish exile in that room. Jews of east and west, religious and secular, wealthy and poor, radical and conservative.
A people dispersed to every corner of the globe, just melting
a little into their surrounds, adopting local language, custom,
dress, before being rudely plucked out and sent onward by
kings and empresses, warlords and clerics, to new lands and
new privations.

The staging of a Zionist assembly in Europe, which unified
Jews of all nationalities, classes, and religious streams under
the banner of a single idea, had been achieved through a combination of grandeur and old-fashioned community organizing. At the First Zionist Congress, also held in Basel in 1897,
Herzl appeared at the Stadtcasino in black trousers, tails, and
a white tie, really more befitting a matinee of *La Traviata* than

---

1 This article originally appeared in the *Jewish Chronicle* on August 13,
   2020.

a Jewish communal event. In the days leading up to the event, Herzl had sat up with students addressing envelopes long into the night.

At that First Congress, a manifesto was adopted that succinctly articulated the aim of Zionism. It was to establish a national home for the Jewish people in the Land of Israel secured under public law. Within this simple declaration stood an almighty mission. The Jews hadn't had a national home for two millennia. The Land of Israel had since 135 CE been known by another name, had seen multiple empires befall it, and had a meager Jewish population of roughly 25,000. Moreover, the mass physical return of a scattered and acculturated people to long vanquished lands was something that had never been achieved in human history.

It was this dreamy idealism that gave Zionism a magnetic quality. It animated Jewish youths to throw themselves into community organizing and intellectual rumbles out of which organised Zionism grew. It led to the founding of grassroots Zionist groups like Bilu (an acronym of the Hebrew phrase meaning "House of Jacob, come ye and let us go"), whose members actually travelled from Tsarist Russia to Palestine and established agricultural settlements. It compelled the likes of Chaim Weizmann to spend his student days in Germany as a member of another Zionist group, the Verein, throwing his humble stipend into sausages and beer while raucously debating Zionism, socialism, nationalism, and internationalism in cafes until the wee hours.

And it prompted the writer Israel Zangwill to lambast the Jewish establishment for seemingly holding back the progress of Zionism to the detriment of the suffering Jewish masses.

Zangwill thundered to a gathering of the Jewish poor in London's East End, "we are supposed to pray three times a day for the return of Jerusalem, but, as soon as we say we want to go back, we are accused of blasphemy!"

When this generation of Jewish activists encountered the pamphlets of thinkers like Leon Pinsker and Herzl, their minds were instantly seared and permanently changed. How could a vigorous, determined young Jew coming of age in a time of unsparing brutality towards Jews, be unmoved by Pinsker's illustration of their stateless people wandering the earth as "a ghost-like apparition of a living corpse . . . living everywhere but nowhere in the correct place"? Or Herzl's functional oratory that promised that "the Jews who wish for a state will have it. We shall live at last as free people on our own soil and die peacefully in our own homes"?

Not only was Zionism exciting and radical, world events conspired to make it a matter of life and death. Jews were forbidden from walking in the rain in Iran for fear that their uncleanliness would wash off to sully Muslim shoes. They were looted, raped, and slaughtered across Russia in 1881 and 1905, in Fez in 1912, and in Shiraz in 1910. This turned Zionism from a rising ideal into an urgent humanitarian mission.

The Kishinev pogrom of 1903, while comparatively less bloody than some of the others of the time, was chronicled so graphically that it caused not only grief but a deep shame in the Jewish world. The poet Hayim Bialik wrote that "in the dark corners of Kishinev, crouching husbands, bridegrooms and brothers peering through the cracks of their shelters, watching their wives, sisters, daughters writhing beneath their bestial defilers, suffocating in their own blood, their flesh portioned out as booty." The *New York Times* reported that "the scenes of horror were beyond description . . . [as] the streets were piled with corpses and wounded." After Kishinev, an editorial of the *American Hebrew* noted that "American Zionism had come of age," while a Christian speaker at a Zionist meeting at Cooper Union declared that, in the wake of Kishinev, "all efforts must be made to establish a Jewish commonwealth." Zionism offered Jews an escape from Kishinev, both physically and psychologically.

Any lingering doubt about the necessity and urgency of Zionism dissipated as the Holocaust descended on Europe. As David Ben-Gurion noted, "what Zionist propaganda for years could not do," that is, to fully reveal Jewish self-delusion and vulnerability, "disaster has done overnight." The surviving Jews, absurdly warehoused in displaced persons camps in Europe several years after the defeat of Nazism, yearned to locate the ruins of their families and try to build new lives away from European antisemitism. "Palestine is definitely and pre-eminently the first choice" for resettlement, Earl Harrison, President Truman's envoy for refugees, reported.

The creation of Israel in May 1948 did nothing to dim Jewish interest in Zionism. The establishment of the state may have been the practical fulfilment of the vision expressed at Basel in 1897, but much work remained. There was the immediate defense of the nascent state from civil war and invasion, the ingathering of exiles, rescue missions for imperilled Jewish communities, the upbuilding of a society, and the pursuit of peace with Arab neighbours once war subsided, a noble goal enshrined in Israel's Declaration of Independence. In a sense, the Zionist project had become even more important as the Jewish world unified behind the goal of creating a society worthy of the two millennia intermission.

For diaspora communities, there were governments to be lobbied to help achieve recognition of Israel and friendly relations with governments and opposition parties, public opinion to shape, humanitarian aid to raise. Zionist organisations like the Jewish National Fund, Women's International Zionist Organization, United Israel Appeal and, a kaleidoscope of others weren't simply folded into the Jewish State in 1948, they redoubled their efforts. There were trees to plant to cultivate the land, university faculties and research institutes to endow, lone soldiers to support, victims of terror to assist, millions of Soviet, African, and Middle Eastern Jews to rescue and absorb. All of this contributed to deepen the investment of diaspora Jews in the Zionist project. No one wanted to miss out on history in the making, and if *aliyah* was impracticable, membership of Zionist organisations, political activism, and fundraising created a sense of unity and belonging enabling diaspora Jews to feel like active players in the extraordinary story of Jewish rehabilitation and national rebirth.

For Jews who had either lapsed in their religious observance or, like the vast majority of Soviet emigres, were never religious to begin with, Zionism offered the same Jewish communal and cultural pride, feelings of belonging, and opportunities for rigorous learning and debate, previously only to be found in religion.

A senior Israeli diplomat once told me that Zionism was his religion. It is the sort of comment that would instantly be misconstrued as amounting to worship of settlements or prayers at the altar of Bibi. But I immediately understood what he meant. He was immersed in the story of Zionism, believed with perfect conviction in its justness and necessity, was inspired by it, and compelled to act civically and humanely by his interpretation of its teachings. He wished to convey the wondrous stories of Zionism to his children—Weizmann's experiments with acetone, Herzl's awakening at the Dreyfus Trial, the magical moment on November 29, 1947 when Jews worldwide realised they would get their state. This diplomat wanted his children to imbibe these stories as he had, so that they too would grow up connected to their Jewishness, know who they are, remain strong in the face of aggressors, and proud in the knowledge that they belong to a people of vision and fortitude.

Yet the price of Israel's incredible success is that those imperatives that drew Jews to Zionism—state building, rescue of Jewish communities, urgent defense—are now seemingly gone, meaning there is much less to make a young Jew of Johannesburg, Sydney, or Toronto feel connected to a national project playing out on the edge of the Mediterranean Sea, and currently devoid of towering figures and spellbinding moments.

The solution is a deeper understanding of what Zionism is and what it truly represents. Zionism, at its core, has always been about rights. Yes, Zionism sought a national home for the Jewish people. But why? To protect the most fundamental right of all, the right to live. Zionism remains, both through its support for a strong Jewish state and its ethos of Jewish resilience and self-help, the greatest bulwark against antisemitism. And it was Zionism that attained recognition that the Jews are a people and thus possess the right to live freely in their own land. As Churchill recognised in 1922, "the Jewish people should know that they are in Palestine as of right and not of sufferance."

History has shown us that the most basic rights extended to other peoples have to be hard won and vigilantly defended when it comes to the Jews. Zionism represents that bundle of rights that the Jews have secured and are unprepared to ever relinquish. The right to a place of refuge and shelter from murderous hatred. The right to a national center for the preservation and enlargement of Jewish cultural, scholarly, and scientific contributions. The right for Jews, like all other nations, to freely determine their own political status.

When expressed as the embodiment of Jewish rights, Zionism soars above party politics and the acrimony of policy-making in modern Israel, and it correctly presents anti-Zionism as a campaign to strip Jews of their rights. But, if Zionism loses a clear purpose and fails to assert what it is for and not merely what it is against, it will be swept away by more emotionally gratifying offerings, which, in reality, have the capacity to deliver absolute ruin.

How Blindness
to Antisemitism
Threatens Parties
and Movements[1]

Keir Starmer, the post-Corbyn leader of the British Labour party, acted swiftly to demote a Member of Parliament who tweeted an article containing a paragraph linking Israel to the killing of George Floyd.[2] In truth, when Labour MP Rebecca Long-Bailey tweeted the interview with the actress Maxine Peake in which she made the appalling and unfounded claim, Long-Bailey may have had no sinister intentions. Indeed, she may have missed the offending paragraph altogether. So common has the obsession with Israel become in the left fringes of social-democratic parties, so accustomed must Long-Bailey be to hearing Israel blamed for all of the world's ills at branch meetings and in her social media feed that a casual reference to the Jewish state masterminding violence on the other side of the world would hardly raise an eyebrow. Instead, Long-Bailey tweeted out the article with no caveats or qualifications,

---

1   This article originally appeared in *Newsweek* on June 30, 2020.

2   Iain Watson, "Labour Anti-Semitism Row: Keir Starmer 'Stands by' Long-Bailey Sacking," BBC News, June 26, 2020.

intervening only to point out that the actress who made the accusation was an "absolute diamond."

The allegation that Israel trains American officers to kneel on the necks of suspects is the sort of half-baked musing one might overhear on a university library lawn. But while such theories often originate on campuses or in the disturbed minds of people like Roger Waters—the musician made the identical claim in a recent interview with a Hamas-affiliated news agency—they rarely stay there.[3] Such theories now have a voice in Congress and in parliaments throughout the world.

This can partly be attributed to the nature of modern communications, which means that fanatical political ideas and prejudices no longer reside in pamphlets that no one outside the movement reads but are now manufactured into compelling content, entirely stripped of context or truth, and instantly directed it into the eyeballs of millions. It is also a symptom of the mainstreaming of once-fringe elements who have shifted from micro-parties, and occasionally the backbenches, to the corridors of power. More than that, it shows how society, stricken by pandemic, discord, and fatigue has embraced conspiratorial thinking.

A common feature of all conspiracies is the belief that something is concealed, that the truth is known only to an enlightened few, and that all our misfortunes are the cause of someone else, some unseen hand that rests upon the levers of power—finance, government, the media. Historically, these delusions have found the Jew to be a suitable enemy. Until

---

3   "Roger Waters: Technique Used in George Floyd's Killing Taught by IDF," *Jerusalem Post*, June 21, 2020.

the mid-twentieth century, the Jews were a stateless people, scattered throughout the world, lacking a cohesiveness and a national center, and therefore both physically vulnerable and uniquely suited to being cast as a mysterious arch-villain in the fantasies of both the far left and the far right. Jewish survival in the face of unparalleled calamites, the ability of the Jews to revive their ancient tongue as a language of everyday use, rebuild scorched communities, and contribute beyond their numbers to the societies in which they live only fed the belief that the Jews were some phantasmic, supernatural presence. They were feared and hated in equal measure.

The Jewish national movement, Zionism, was supposed to render all that irrelevant. By being rescued from exile and restored to a national home approximating the territories they controlled in ancient times, the Jews should have attained equality with other peoples who had homelands, flags, distinct languages, national traditions, and the rest. But so deeply ingrained was the characterisation of the Jews and so compelling is the desire to blame a despised other for our own failings, that the return of the Jews to their homeland nearly two millennia after their expulsion by the Romans, an event unprecedented in human history, was not universally greeted with wonder and admiration. Rather, it spawned new feelings of loathing and hardened the perception that this people were bound up in something suspiciously extraordinary, even supernatural.

In fact, far from curing antisemitism and the conspiracy theories that so often give effect to it, Zionism and the State of Israel offered a new medium through which to express irrational feelings towards the Jews. As Nazi-era race theories about immutable Jewish inferiority were completely discredited and older religion-based contempt for the Jews lacked relevance in contemporary times, particularly among the secular hard left, Zionism and Israel became the new outlets for those driven to apoplexy by Jewish assertiveness, perceived success, and stubborn refusal to submit and disappear. Pseudo-political accusations of genocide, ethnic cleansing, apartheid, collective punishment replaced classical accusations of ritual murder, bloodlust, a cunning malevolence, and being a people who stands in the way of a better world.

It is this modern politicisation of antisemitism that ensured that Rebecca Long-Bailey, who would have been instantly awake to a racist jibe directed at any other minority group, could mistake the antisemitism in the interview for benign criticism of a state she doesn't much care for.

The belief that every injustice can be traced to Israeli evil was perhaps best demonstrated by another British Labour politician (now mercifully retired) Clare Short, who claimed during a pro-Palestinian conference in Brussels in 2007 that not only was Israel "much worse than the original apartheid state," but that it "undermines the international community's reaction to global warming."[4] Given Short's conclusion that global warming could "end the human race," one can readily connect the dots about how loathsome and threatening Israel must be and what should be done with it. For good measure, Israel has also been accused of causing domestic violence in Gaza

---

4   Daniel Schwammenthal, "The Israel-Bashing Club," *Wall Street Journal*, September 3, 2007.

as passionate Palestinian men have no choice but to beat their wives to assert their masculinity in the face of Israeli aggression.[5]

More recently, Black Lives Matter, a group ostensibly formed to combat racism, adopted a manifesto[6] that, amidst the discourse on incarceration rates, police conduct, and racial profiling, also accuses Israel of being an "apartheid state" and committing "genocide" of the Palestinians, whose population throughout the Holy Land has undergone a continuous and spectacular increase since the advent of modern Zionism in the nineteenth century. The UK arm of the movement then paused in its tweets on black lives to spray off an anti-Israel medley including offering its weighty legal opinion that Israel is in breach of international law and lamenting the "gagging" of attacks on Zionism.

The campaign to attach Zionism to every grievance and injustice has its origins in Stalin's deteriorating mind during the last years of his reign. It became the basis for official Soviet anti-Zionism and remains as a vestige in far-left political movements today. But, in a sense, it runs even deeper than that. It is the hallmark of an irrational, fanatical mind, incapable of grasping the nuance and complexity of life. Just as traditional antisemitism brought ruin and misery, anti-Zionism will corrupt noble movements and worthy causes unless it is finally stamped out.

---

5   Danielle Ziri, "Israel Slams UN Report Blaming It for Domestic Abuse of Palestinian Women," *Jerusalem Post*, March 8, 2016, updated March 9, 2016.

6   Emma Green, "Why Do Black Activists Care About Palestine?," *Atlantic*, August 18, 2016.

Lest We Forget?
Seventy-Five Years after
Auschwitz Plenty Do[1]

On the eve of the seventy-fifth anniversary of the liberation of the Auschwitz death camp, a new study has found that a quarter of French millennials haven't heard of the Holocaust,[2] while an earlier study of American millennials found that sixty-six percent did not know what Auschwitz was.[3]

The findings come at a time of surging antisemitism in both countries, with incidents targeting French Jews rising by seventy-four percent, while the United States has seen a series of lethal attacks targeting Jewish gatherings and places of worship, the latest involving a machete attack at the home of a rabbi in upstate New York.[4] In Australia, serious incidents of

1   This article originally appeared in the *Sydney Morning Herald* on January 26, 2020.
2   "Stunning Survey of French Adults Reveals Critical Gaps in Holocaust Knowledge," Claims Conference, https://www.claimscon.org/france-study/.
3   Julie Zauzmer, "Holocaust Study: Two-Thirds of Millennials Don't Know what Auschwitz Is," *Washington Post*, April 12, 2018.
4   Yael Halon, "New York Rabbi whose Home was Scene of Machete Attack Speaks Out: 'We will Forge Forward in Faith,'" *Fox News*, December 29, 2019.

antisemitic verbal abuse, intimidation, and harassment rose by thirty percent in the past year.[5]

The fact so many young people have no knowledge of a genocide conducted in the heart of enlightened Europe, in part through the operation of the most lethal and efficient killing facility in human history, is disturbing in itself. The consequences of this absence of knowledge will surely be felt for years to come. It is a challenging story to teach, harder still to fully imbibe, but one that is critical to understanding man's destructive capacity, the endpoint of the relentless debasing of a people, and the misery that racism can unleash on the world.

Over 1.3 million people were murdered at Auschwitz, ninety percent of them Jews. By the time the genocide of the Jews across Europe had ended, more than three million Jews had been killed in the death camps. The total Jewish dead stood in the vicinity of six million. They died in all corners of Europe, from disease in ghettos, from poison gas, mass shootings, live burial, beatings, incineration.

78% of the Jews who had lived in territories that fell to the Nazis perished. In comparison, between 1.4% to 3% of the non-Jewish population in the same territory was killed. Dynasties and entire families, great sages and common workers, Nobel laureates and humble students, whole villages and communities, all disappeared. Thriving Jewish intellectual and cultural centers like Krakow and Vilnius that had bustled with

---

5   The ECAJ 2019 Antisemitism Report, November 24, 2019, Executive Council of Australian Jewry, https://www.ecaj.org.au/the-ecaj-2019-antisemitism-report/.

Jewish life were now reduced to rude husks, urban memorials of human depravity.

How many more Freuds and Einsteins, Chagalls and Primo Levis were among them, we can never know. A million Jewish children were killed. A million Anne Franks vanished in a pit of suffering.

But the numbers obscure the millions of individual stories of cruelty, misery, and unbearable loss. While the precise manner of the killings was so bestial that it forces one to reconsider the very nature of humanity.

The Jews were taken to the camps in train wagons used for transporting cattle in which they would ride across the continent for days on end, completely without food or water, sometimes given a pause so that the corpses of loved ones could be tossed out of the wagons before continuing onward to the camps.

In some camps, the fit were put to slave labor until their bodies gave out, while the very young, the old, and the sick were selected for gassing immediately. The process of selection would take place on the platform immediately upon arrival. Nazi doctors looked over the human cargo, sending them to one queue or another, forever tearing sister from sister, mother from child.

The ones selected to die immediately were led into chambers that were sealed behind them before canisters of poison were released through chutes in the ceiling. When the victims ceased their writhing and their nervous systems succumbed, other inmates were charged with transferring the dead to the crematoria, clearing the chamber of visible signs of distress like bodily waste and fingernails clawed into walls, to ensure the next batch of victims would enter the chamber without disorder or resistance. At the peak of the killing, the Jews were made unalive at a rate of up to 15,000 people a day.[6]

At Auschwitz, human experiments were conducted on the living, including determining the time to death from injection with various poisons, the effect of removal of organs without anaesthetic; and freezing victims to see how close they could be brought to the point of death and still be revived. If they survived the torture that masqueraded as science, their only salvation was the gas chamber.

Those who were able to survive for any length of time in the camps existed in a realm somewhere between life and death, but surely closer to death. They ate virtually nothing, slept in barns, worked outdoors in the freezing Polish winter wrapped in rags, and were rife with diseases like dysentery and typhoid from malnutrition and the absence of clean water. Such was the deathly pall about them that rats sometimes attacked the still living, mistaking them for corpses.

In the perfect crescendo to centuries of gradually reducing the humanity of the Jewish people, they were exterminated in purpose-built camps, industrial factories of destruction, using a common pesticide, Zyklon-B.

The seemingly infinite stories of infinite evil and suffering that together form the Holocaust have been presented to us over and over again in dispassionate historical texts, in Hollywood films, novellas, and memoirs. All seek and all fail

---

6   Doyle Rice, "15,000 Murders a Day: August-October 1942 were the Holocaust's Deadliest Months," *USA Today*, January 2, 2019, updated January 9, 2019.

to fully explain why human beings would act this way to their fellow man. What discord exists in the hearts of ordinary men and women that they would shed their humanity entirely and seize with unrelenting fury and purpose the opportunity to dispossess, humiliate, and destroy their neighbors simply because they were Jewish? This is the imponderable at the heart of the Holocaust. And yet, as incomplete as our powers to fully comprehend this story may be, through the study of it, we develop an empathy, a greater humanity, and an awareness of our own capacity to destroy.

Perhaps then, stories of Australian schoolchildren taunting their Jewish peers as "vermin,"[7] or of the insignia of Nazi killing squads being proudly displayed at nationalist rallies,[8] or the flag of the Nazi regime being hoisted in a Victorian town for all to see[9] can be consigned to the dustbin of history.

7   Rossella Tercatin, "Mummy, I'm a Jewish Rodent:' 5-Year-Old Aussie after Antisemitic Attacks," *Jerusalem Post*, October 5, 2019.

8   Samantha Maiden, "Fraser Anning: Nazis, What Nazis? I Didn't See Any in St Kilda," *New Daily*, January 6, 2019, updated January 7, 2019.

9   Sean Wales and Leonie Thorne, "Nazi Flag Taken Down amid Calls to Strengthen Anti-Vilification Laws," ABC News, January 14, 2020, updated January 16, 2020.

Red Terror—How the Soviet Union Shaped Modern Anti-Zionist Discourse[1]

The Arab-Israeli conflict traverses decades, manifests in regular wars, terrorism, and endless political skirmishes in international forums. It is also a battle to establish narratives—victims and aggressors, Davids and Goliaths, oppressors and oppressed. Language and the meaning given to basic concepts form a key part of this battle. It is easy for the Jewish people to establish a claim to the territory known as Judea and Samaria, whereas the later formulation "West Bank," coined by the Jordanians following their occupation of the area in 1948, is a bland geographic descriptor that strips the territory of its historical significance. The Associated Press recently stumbled into the morass of political language when it declined to identify the men who tortured and killed Israeli athletes at the Munich Olympic Games in 1972 as Palestinian terrorists, instead calling them "guerillas" and "gunmen." And there is no term in the vernacular of the conflict that is misapplied and distorted more than "Zionism."

---

1   This piece was originally published by the Australian Institute of International Affairs on September 10, 2019.

Zionism, correctly understood, refers simply to a return of the Jewish people to "Zion," one of several names given to Jerusalem and the surrounding lands in which the Jews lived and governed in ancient times. In the late nineteenth century, the idea of a Jewish national return to those lands shifted from a seemingly intangible ideal, a wistful age-old expression of yearning for freedom, to a precise, secular, political movement.

The aim of Zionism was to reconstitute a Jewish state in the territory the Jews knew as "Eretz Yisrael" (the Land of Israel), and which had been renamed "Palestine" following the suppression of the final Jewish rebellion by the Roman Emperor Hadrian in the year 135 CE. The Balfour Declaration, United Nations General Assembly Resolution 181 (II), and a succession of binding instruments of international law from the San Remo Resolution to the League of Nations Mandate for Palestine had all recognized that the Jews were a distinct people with an unbroken connection to the land and a right to reform their state in some part of that land.

Zionism therefore was the foundational movement of the modern State of Israel. As such, those determined to erase an autonomous Jewish presence from the Middle East have assessed that, if they can succeed in depicting Zionism as something loathsome and unjust, the case for Israel can be dramatically undermined.

The contemporary campaign to distort the meaning of Zionism and to associate it with popular concepts of evil largely has its origins in the rapid deterioration of Soviet-Israeli relations, which conditioned attitudes to Israel in the political left.

Zionism was once celebrated by the left as an organic movement of national return and a model for national liberation and decolonization movements throughout the world.

Israel's victory in its War of Independence and refusal to succumb to far mightier foes was positively awe-inspiring to adherents of political movements predicated on toppling structures of power. As chronicled by Philip Mendes in his study of Zionism and the political left, "all international communist parties supported partition and the creation of a Jewish State." The US Communist Party called Israel "an organic part of the world struggle for peace and democracy," while the French Communists viewed the Jewish fighters as the comrades of resistance fighters throughout the world.

But as Israel charted its own course, emerged from its wars economically and militarily superior to the Arabs, and became more ambitious and assertive in how it conducted its security affairs, the support of the Soviet Union and of the international left entered a sharp decline, followed by a complete reversal.

As the Cold War set in, Israel's first prime minister, David Ben-Gurion, assured the US ambassador that Israel was "western in its orientation, its people are democratic, and realise that only through the co-operation and support of the US can they become strong and remain free."

Israel's "western orientation" became abundantly clear to the Soviet Union when it joined Britain and France in the Suez Campaign in 1956 to liberate a key maritime route linking Asia to Europe amidst threats to nationalize the canal by Egypt's President Gamal Abdel Nasser, a key Soviet ally.

The campaign, seen by Moscow as a direct threat to its strategic power in the Middle East, sent the Soviets into a state of foaming apoplexy, resulting in threats to deploy nuclear weapons against the British and French and to annihilate Israel entirely.

The Soviet Union had already cut diplomatic relations with Israel in February 1953, only weeks before the death of Stalin and after a period of rapid escalation of state antisemitism, culminating in the notorious "Doctors' Plot," in which Jewish doctors in the Soviet Union were accused of plotting to poison party officials.

Soon the state media was saturated with anti-Zionist propaganda, depicting bloated, hook-nosed Jewish bankers and all-consuming serpents embossed with the Star of David.

Anti-Zionism had become virtually indistinguishable from antisemitism. As the British political theorist Alan Johnson observed, "what 'the Jew' once was in older antisemitism—uniquely malevolent, full of blood lust, all-controlling, the hidden hand, tricksy, always acting in bad faith, the obstacle to a better, purer, more spiritual world, uniquely deserving of punishment, and so on—the Jewish state now is. . . ."

In time, these depictions would reach not only the Soviet reader but, through Soviet satellites in Europe, South America, and the Middle East, and through communist parties and publications throughout the world, these ideas would nestle in far-left circles in the West, including political parties, human rights organizations, militant trade unions, and, of course, campuses.

The propaganda was highly compelling and steeped in long-established themes of Jewish bloodthirstiness, greed, corruption, manipulation, and cunning. It would contend that the very existence of a Jewish homeland was not only a plot of imperialism, but a mortal danger to the peace of the world.

It was what Hitler called the "big lie"—the use of dramatically overblown fiction to deceive the public. Hitler, the supreme propagandist, observed that the bigger the lie the more believable it was: "It would never come into people's heads to fabricate colossal untruths, and they would not believe that others could have the impudence to distort the truth so infamously. . . ."

The big lies about Zionism would soon find their way into the most influential forums in the world. When a sub-commission of the United Nations was tasked with drafting a convention on the "elimination of all forms of racial discrimination," the proceedings naturally focused on apartheid, neo-Nazism, and antisemitism. But the Soviets viewed the reference to antisemitism as a direct rebuke to their anti-Jewish measures, and served up an amendment that "was almost a joke," even to the Soviet delegation itself.

The amendment inserted Zionism into the listed forms of racism. According to sources close to the deliberations, the Soviets understood "full well that the idea that Zionism is racism is an indefensible position," yet they floated it anyway, in part to turn the US-led initiative into farce and in part, perhaps, to see how far a "big lie" could go.

Ultimately, the convention was adopted with neither antisemitism nor Zionism referred to—the ploy had worked. But the seed has been planted.

Then, on November 10, 1975, the General Assembly of the United Nations passed Resolution 3379 on the "elimination of all forms of racial discrimination," which determined that "Zionism is a form of racism and discrimination."

The US ambassador to the United Nations, Patrick Moynihan, called the Resolution "a great evil" that had given "the abomination of antisemitism the appearance of international sanction."

The proposition that the Jewish emancipation movement was actually a form of racism, now declared to be truth by the United Nations, could then be used to purge mainstream Jewish voices from liberal campaigns and civil society organizations.

In 1977, student unions across Britain debated motions along the lines of Resolution 3379. York, Salford, Warwick, and Lancaster went further, passing motions to expel their Jewish societies "on the grounds that they are Zionist and therefore racist."

The concept of denying platforms to fascist and white supremacist speakers on university campuses was now being applied to stifle mainstream voices who expressed support for the State of Israel.

Moynihan foresaw this. An earlier UN resolution had, at the instigation of the Soviet Union, viewed "racism to be merely a form of Nazism." It followed that, if racism was merely a form of Nazism and Zionism is a form of racism, then Zionism is a form of Nazism.

On this basis, anti-Zionist students could harass Zionists and be seen as taking a noble stand against Nazism. This twisted logic was applied by anti-Israel students at Sydney University in 2015 when they attempted to stop the public lecture of a retired British colonel for his earlier statements in support of Israel. And by the organizers of the Chicago Dyke March who blocked Jewish participants from marching with Stars of David on the basis that Zionism was a form of "white supremacism."

The theme of Jews becoming the new Nazis, a double blow that associates Zionism with supreme evil and mocks the victims of the Holocaust by equating them with their murderers, has become a mainstay of anti-Zionist discourse.

In a conflict as deep-seated and volatile as this, it may seem like a trifling pursuit to seek to restore accurate meaning to terminology. But there can be no hope for peaceful coexistence between Israelis and Palestinians so long as the movement on which Israel was established seven decades ago, the movement that expresses Jewish hopes and Jewish rights, is so poorly understood and so successfully distorted.

The Memory of the Holocaust and the Mystery of Unfathomable Evil[1]

It is an honor for me to speak on this day, in this place, and to do so in the presence of so many distinguished guests, particularly the survivors of the greatest crime in history.

The Holocaust, the term given to the industrial-scale slaughter of the Jews of Europe, is often examined in isolation. An event without precedent and without successor. Certainly, the enormity of the killing, the unsparing barbarity and cool sophistication with which it was carried out, and its genesis in the center of enlightened Western Europe all contribute to its uniqueness. This in turn means that the Holocaust is largely viewed as an aberration, a deviation in the progression of human history.

But in reality, the events of the Holocaust were entirely predictable and were shown to the Jews in preview over and over again.

---

1   This is the transcription of the keynote speech for Holocaust Remembrance Day, given in Queensland, Australia, on May 5, 2019.

The expulsion of the Jews from Spain and England in the Middle Ages showed how dispensable this ancient nation was. The massacre of Jews in York in 1190 and Odesa in 1905 showed how easily a mob could be compelled to kill men, women, and children in a great release of pent-up frustration in times of political upheaval or economic downturn. The Kishinev pogrom during which the local police looked on as Jews were defiled and killed showed that, at best, police units would stand aside for the mob, at worst they would *be* the mob. And the Cossack Rebellion led by Bogdan Chmelnytsky in seventeenth-century Ukraine in which hundreds of thousands of Jews were tortured and killed demonstrated the sadism, vulgarity, and blood revelry that abounds in seemingly ordinary men.

How fickle are the rules and laws we establish, the order we think we have, the norms and customs we expect to be followed, when faced with overwhelming evil backed by unstoppable force.

But the horrors of the past were not taken as harbingers of worse to come but of evidence that, no matter how dire the outlook, this too would surely pass. But this did not pass. Despite the history, despite the warnings, in the years before the Holocaust, the Jews of Europe continued to live in a state of perfect self-delusion, on the precipice of a complete inferno.

Before the Nazis could begin the process of ghettoizing, deporting, and then murdering millions of Jews spread across hundreds of communities in Europe, they had to overcome enormous practical challenges such as defining who was a Jew, accounting for products of mixed marriages and conversions, identifying Jews, many of whom were highly assimilated, and gradually expunging the Jews from visibility such that their coming demise would barely raise a whimper. This all required as much bureaucratic diligence as ruthless inhumanity.

In the end, the Germans overcame every single challenge with an almost impressive focus and enterprise. The Nazis also demonstrated a truly extraordinary understanding of human nature.

They correctly posited that the level of hatred for the Jews was such that they could be systematically stripped of all rights, removed from the wider population, robbed blind, and eventually murdered with little or no public reaction, particularly when done under the cover of war.

For this, the Germans had their antisemitic predecessors to thank. The Roman Empire, the Church with its marauding Crusaders, nationalist figures like Chmelnytsky, intellectual titans like Martin Luther had all imprinted in the European psyche a characterization of the Jew as subhuman. He was cunning yet parasitic, ritualistically clean but plainly filthy, lazy yet all-powerful, studious yet utterly perverse. And always inferior and, most importantly, unchangeable.

Full of paradoxes, unsupported by fact or reason, this depiction of the Jews over centuries fed the human urge to see and understand evil and to find a cause for life's horrors and misfortunes.

And, to allow otherwise decent and moral people to descend into such loathing for their fellow man, it had been necessary to not only completely dehumanize the Jew, to reduce him to the status of a flea, but to also frame any action against him as a helpless resort to self-defense against a nation of parasites and murderers.

Martin Luther had called the Jews "thirsty bloodhounds and murderers of all Christendom" that had "poisoned water and wells, stolen children, and torn and hacked them apart." "Christians have been tortured and persecuted by the Jews all over the world," Luther said.

In 1895, decades before the world had heard of Hitler, the speaker of the German parliament called the Jews "cholera germs."

And what is left to be done with such a thing but to destroy it? As the Holocaust historian Yehuda Bauer said, "One does not argue with parasites."

As total war descended on Europe, the fact that the Jews were literally disappearing was of very little concern.

Their vast personal and communal possessions were harvested, they were confined physically to ghettoes where they were forced to live as the insular, diseased wretched race that propaganda had said they were all along, and from there they were eventually taken to be killed—men, women, children.

The process of mass extermination began in June 1941 after the invasion of the Soviet Union. The initial method of killing was through mobile killing squads, known as *Einsatzgruppen*, that moved on the heels of the advancing German army. Their mission was to comb the cities and towns for Jews.

The *Einsatzgruppen* units would move with devastating speed, trapping the large Jewish population centers before the victims could discover their fate, then returning to conduct further sweeps, sometimes days later, sometimes weeks later, but they would always return to ensnare any Jews who had evaded the initial dragnet.

By the war's end, some two million Jews would be killed in massacres in forest and ravines. Every village, every town, every city in the former Soviet Union would have its own killing field.

In Romania, the locals grew impatient by the orderly manner in which the Germans were developing the killing process and took matters into their own hands.

In Bucharest, Jews, among them a five-year-old girl, were taken to a kosher slaughterhouse, skinned alive, and hung from meat hooks.

In Bogdanovka, nearly 5000 sick and infirm Jews were crammed into barns and stables which were the sprinkled with straw, doused in gasoline, and set alight.

The Jews of Jedbawne in Poland were similarly shut into a barn and incinerated alive by their Polish neighbors.

In Budapest, 20,000 Jews were assembled on the bank of the River Danube and shot, toppling into the waters beneath.

The first gassing of Jews took place at the Chelmno camp in Poland. From December 1941, transportations to the camp commenced, where the Jews were loaded into vans specially rigged and sealed so as to direct the exhaust fumes into the cabin. The victims were driven for around ten minutes by which time they died by asphyxiation and the corpses were then taken directly to pre-prepared mass graves in the adjacent Waldiger forest.

By the end of the war, some 320,000 Jews would be murdered at Chelmno.

Other camps in Poland, Belzec, Sobibor, Treblinka, Maidanek, Auschwitz-Birkenau commenced operating as factories of death after January 1942, following the formal adoption, at the Wannsee Conference in Berlin, of the plan to completely exterminate the Jews, in what came to be known as the "final solution to the Jewish problem."

With the camps built and the methods of mass killing perfected, the ghettoes of Europe could be liquidated. The Jews were crammed into train cars used for transporting cattle in which they would ride across the continent for days on end, completely without food or water, given an occasional pause at which the human waste and corpses of loved ones could be tossed out of the cars before continuing onward to the camps.

In some camps, the fit were used as slave labor until their bodies gave out, while the very young, the old, and the sick were selected for gassing immediately. The process of selection would take place on the platform immediately upon arrival. Nazi doctors looked over the human cargo, sending them to one queue or another, forever tearing sister from sister, parent from child.

The ones selected to die immediately were led into chambers that were sealed behind them before canisters of poison were released through chutes in the ceiling. When the victims ceased their writhing and their nervous systems succumbed, other inmates were charged with transferring the dead to the crematoria and clearing the chamber of visible signs of distress such as fingernails clawed into walls, to ensure the next batch of victims would enter the chamber without disorder or resistance.

At Auschwitz, human experiments were conducted on the living, including determining the time to death from injection with various poisons, the effect of removal of organs without anesthetic; and freezing victims to see how close they could be brought to the point of death and still be revived. If they survived the torture that masqueraded as science, their only salvation was the gas chamber.

Those who were able to survive for any length of time in the camps existed in a realm somewhere between life and death, but surely closer to death. They ate virtually nothing, slept in barns, worked outdoors in the freezing Polish winter wrapped in rags, and were rife with diseases like dysentery and typhoid from malnutrition and the absence of clean water.

They could have only lived from one moment to the next in the knowledge that their families had been killed and that the same fate would strike them at any time. Such was the deathly pall about them that rats sometimes attacked the still living, mistaking them for corpses.

In the perfect crescendo to centuries of gradually debasing and reducing the humanity of the Jewish people, the Jews were exterminated in purpose-built camps, industrial facilities of destruction, using a common pesticide, Zyklon-B, at a rate of up to 15,000 people a day.

When the Germans were finally forced into retreat, they abandoned the camps, deploying inmates to hastily conceal the apparatus of industrial death as best they could, before killing off the remaining inmates or else sending them on long, winter death marches to other camps.

By the time the killing had ended, more than three million had died in the camps. The total Jewish dead stood in the vicinity of six million. They died from disease in ghettos, from poison gas, mass shootings, live burial, beatings, burning alive. Half of the dead were from Poland, a country in which Jewish life had accounted for some ten percent of the total population. They had perished in all corners of Europe from the Baltic to France, from Scandinavia to the Balkans.

In 1939, Europe was home to 9.5 million Jews. By war's end, nearly sixty-five percent of those Jews were dead.

Dynasties and entire families, great sages and common workers, Nobel laureates and humble students, babies, pensioners, whole villages and communities had all disappeared. Thriving Jewish intellectual and cultural centers like Krakow and Vilnius that had bustled with Jewish life—seminary students, merchants, families, all manner of artisans—were now reduced to rude husks, urban memorials of human depravity.

The Jews' possessions were now divvied up between the Nazi conquerors and the locals, the former inhabitants now piles of ash in the forests surrounding the camps.

How many more Freuds and Einsteins, Chagalls and Primo Levis were among them we can never know. A million Jewish children were killed. A million Anne Franks vanished in a pit of suffering.

Compounding the Jewish sense of helplessness and betrayal was the collective shrug of indifference that was the overwhelming reaction of the international community before, during, and after the slaughter.

When Franklin Roosevelt convened a conference in Evian, France to discuss the question of Jewish refugees following Germany's annexation of Austria in 1938, the conference broke up with no solution to the looming crisis.

Capturing the mood of pathetic diplomatic indifference, the Australian representative, T. W. White, explained that Australia would not be taking Jewish refugees: "As we have no real racial problem, we are not desirous of importing one," as though the Nazi persecution of the Jews was really just a disagreement between communities.

A German observer at the conference reported to the Nazi top brass that "the many speeches and discussions show that with the exception of a few countries that can still admit Jewish emigrants, there is an extensive aversion to a significant flow of emigrants either out of social considerations or out of an unexpressed racial abhorrence against Jewish emigrants." Hitler was said to have drawn the conclusion from the conference that he could do with the Jews exactly as he pleased.

The killings continued even after the fall of Nazi Germany and the liberation of Europe. In Kielce, Poland in 1946, a mob, which included hundreds of mills workers, set upon Jewish Holocaust survivors, clubbing forty-two to death. There were reports of Jews being killed while attempting to return to their homes across Poland. In August 1945, thunderous applause greeted the passing of a resolution by the Polish Peasants Party thanking Hitler for destroying the Jews and calling for the expulsion of any survivors.

The dehumanization of the Jews had been so complete that even the disaster that antisemitism had unleashed on the European continent, the bestial carnage to which millions bore witness, could not dislodge it.

The people of Europe had allowed themselves to believe that their misfortune, their poverty, their war losses, their poor crops, and their national debt were squarely the fault of the Jew. The Jewish peasants tending the land, the pious, secluded families seeking wisdom in ancient texts, the middle-class merchants of the cities, the teachers, the drunks, the scholars, the poets, the vagrants, the bankers, and the children. In the final wash it just didn't matter how absurd the idea of their collective guilt was. The die had been cast over hundreds of years.

The people believed this lunacy because they wanted to believe it. And if they were wrong and they had just extinguished millions of lives for no reason at all and war and poverty and misfortune would not go to the grave with the Jew, well, at least they have blown off a little steam and enriched themselves in the process.

The Holocaust brought no redemption or awakening. Its seemingly infinite stories of infinite evil have been presented to us over and over again in dispassionate historical texts, in Hollywood films, novellas, and memoirs. All seek, and all fail to fully explain why human beings would act this way to their fellow man.

What was it about the Jews that aroused such feeling that the army of a sophisticated nation would be deployed to traverse the European continent with the mission of ending every final Jewish life? What discord existed in the hearts of ordinary men and women that they would shed their humanity entirely and seize with unrelenting fury and purpose the opportunity to dispossess, humiliate, and destroy their neighbors simply because they were Jewish? These are the imponderables at the heart of the Holocaust.

The popular slogan to emerge after it was "Never Again." This has been variously interpreted to mean everything from "never again will the Jews go like lambs to the slaughter" to "never again will humanity allow the evil of antisemitism to take root" to "never again will the world stand by and allow a people to all but vanish."

But in the mere seventy-five years that have passed since the end of the Holocaust, in a period when many of the victims remain alive to bear witness, we have seen the increasing popularity of Holocaust denial, denial of the very event itself, a denial that our people ever lived and died.

We have seen new genocide in Darfur and Cambodia, Srenbrenica and Rwanda, we have seen antisemitism arise with fresh vigor, and, in our very days, Jews are targeted for being Jews in our homes, in our synagogues, in our schools, even in our graves.

But it may be that, just as the Holocaust is not a single story but a collection of millions of individual moments of trauma, horror, and pain, there is not a single lesson to be drawn from it. Rather, we should each strive to take something from it as individuals.

For me, that something is a deep love for the Jewish people, a determination to preserve and defend the memories of our sacred dead, and a commitment to never relinquish what was gifted to me and what was so cruelly taken from our martyrs—the ability to live freely and live proudly as a Jew.

To Jerusalem
and Back[1]

I land at Ben-Gurion Airport just before midnight and begin the long ascent to Jerusalem. The headiness hits me immediately and will remain until I depart ten days later. A few hours later I sit bleary-eyed at breakfast ahead of a day spent trading ideas with some of Israel's finest intellects from diplomacy, journalism, and academia.

I take lunch with the Director-General of the Foreign Ministry Yuval Rotem, former ambassador to Australia. A perfect specimen of energy meeting acumen, sneeringly called "cunning" by Bob Carr in his diaries, Yuval at once sees the big picture while recalling the smallest detail.

In the evening, I dine on Kurdish dumplings and hummus while discussing war and peace with a spokesman for the Israeli Prime Minister.

The following morning I depart for the Palestinian Territories to visit a Palestinian refugee camp, meet the mayor of Bethlehem, and venture into darkest Hebron.

I enter the camp, really just a common village of paved roads and stone houses, the entrance to which is adorned by an enormous key symbolizing the Palestinian quest to return

---

1   This article originally appeared in the *Spectator* on June 9, 2018.

to what is now Israel. The enormity of the key aptly captures the degree to which the Palestinians are anchored in the past, unable to conceive of a future. Everywhere I turn I see the images of their "martyrs." A corflute shows a young man with a Hamas headband and the smouldering wreck of an Israeli passenger bus he detonated. Where I come from such people are considered the lowest of cowards whose names should be blotted out. Here their names are exalted.

Next—the mayor of Bethlehem. A great walrus of a man, he enthusiastically shakes my hand no fewer than six times. We discuss the peace process, Rabin, Olmert, Sharon. I am impressed by his reasonableness. As he speaks, I picture EU officials leaving his company beaming to one another, "now there's a man you can do business with!" But the longer he talks without interjection the more his stream of consciousness takes him down avenues of delusion and conspiracy.

On my way out, the mayor's elegant young deputy diverts me to the balcony overlooking Manger Square. She speaks of her desire to live in peace and freedom. Her eyes flash with such intense passion that a lesser Zionist would have crumbled and given her east Jerusalem right there and then.

In Hebron I stand at the spot where a Palestinian sniper shot a ten-month-old baby girl as she lay in her stroller. I inspect the shuttered shops of Shuhada Street and squeeze past queuing Palestinian men, their faces fixed with simmering rage, chanting "Allahu Akhbar" while waiting at a checkpoint to pray at the Cave of the Patriarchs. The indignity of being made to queue by young Jews in fatigues is clear, but then nothing in Hebron is simple and everything is conditioned by bloody history.

I stop to speak to a young soldier heading for the front line. His nervous energy is palpable. I wish him strength. As I leave Hebron I hear the rhythmic thuds of tear gas rounds.

The following day I spend with Sharren Haskel, a rising star of the Israeli Parliament, whose intense passion matches that of the young PLO official on the balcony over Bethlehem. She invites me to attend a Memorial Day ceremony in Itamar, deep in the West Bank.

Itamar means one thing to me—the Fogel family. In 2011, two cousins from the Arab village of Awarta penetrated the perimeter fence of Itamar, broke into the home of the Fogel family, and hacked Ruth and Ehud Fogel to death in their beds before killing their three children. Three-month-old Hadas Fogel was decapitated in her cot.

Sharren warns me that some will surely disapprove of a Jewish leader spending Memorial Day in the settlements. But on a day to mourn the Jewish dead, I couldn't care less what side of a defunct armistice line they died on, and I can think of no worthier place to be than the home of the Fogels.

We drive through the exquisite countryside of the West Bank—biblical and bucolic. The ceremony begins. We bake in the hilltop sun. The mood is sombre and pained. Teenagers recite prayers for the fallen, community leaders weep as they deliver their addresses, and a kid strums a guitar while his friend in a knitted *kippa* sings beautiful lamentations. My attention is seized by a short, stocky man who shuffles to the podium before reciting the prayer for the dead (*Kaddish*). He has the face of a broken man, of one whose pain is fresh. The father of a recently fallen soldier perhaps.

When the ceremony concludes, Sharren mingles with the people while I stand back and take in the majesty of the surrounds and the weight of the moment. Sharren walks over with the man from the podium and introduces him to me as Boaz Shabo. It's a name I have heard but cannot immediately place. He tells me how much it means to him that I came. I am humbled. "Come, I want to show you," he tells me, leading me to a huddled group of people obscuring a monument of some sort. They part reverentially for Boaz and I see four identical graves littered with small stones left by mourners. "This is my wife, Rachel, and these are our three sons." Before there was the Fogel family there was the Shabo family. As Boaz worked late one evening, terrorists broke into his home and murdered his wife and their three children, the youngest a boy of five. Boaz and I lock in a long embrace and I wish him strength and long life.

In my remaining days in Israel I catch up with the leader of the Israeli opposition, Isaac "Bougie" Herzog, and meet Tzipi Livni to discuss peace and the Palestinians, and join a mission of the Jewish Diplomatic Corps.

I leave the country dizzier still from the beauty of its soulful people, the splendor of the land, the scale of the nation's achievements, and the enormity of its threats. I think of the grandeur of Jerusalem. Most of all, I think about Boaz Shabo's tormented face and the price of having a Jewish state. Indeed, the price of being Jewish.

As I wait to check my bags at Ben-Gurion Airport, I flick through stories about Boaz. Five years after the massacre he remarried and two years later, after losing his three sons to terrorists, his second wife gave him triplets. "Never give in to despair. There is always a light at the top, even if it might involve a hard climb," Boaz told the papers after the birth. And therein lies the story of the Jewish people and the destiny of their tiny nation-state. Strength, defiance, and progress. Eyes fixed to the future while never forgetting the lessons of the past.

How a Poet and a Composer Overcame Soviet Censorship of the Holocaust[1]

From the late 1950s, a small group of Soviet intellectuals began assembling annually at a site on the outskirts of the Ukrainian capital, Kyiv, that had become a pasture for cattle. Some would stand in solemn lament, while the Jews among them would in hushed incantations speak the ancient prayer for the dead. The Soviet police would look on. If the group lingered for too long or began to arouse the interest of passersby, they would be dispersed. If they laid flowers, they would spend the next fifteen days in jail.

On September 19, 1961 another Soviet intellectual, Yevgeny Yevtushenko, published a poem bearing the name of that site in the leading Soviet literary journal, *Literaturnaya Gazeta*. The poem was *Babi Yar*.[2] It began with the words, "No

---

1   This article originally appeared in Tablet Magazine on September 16, 2017.

2   The site is known as "Babyn Yar" in Ukrainian and "Babi Yar" in Russian. Yevtushenko's poem was written in Russian, hence "Babi Yar" is used in this article when quoting or referring to the poem and the subsequent symphony but "Babyn Yar" when referring to the site.

monument stands over Babi Yar. A steep cliff only, like the rudest headstone."

The site, a sprawling ravine four miles from the center of Kyiv, was the scene of one of the darkest chapters in human history, an oft-forgotten and deliberately obfuscated stanza in the chronicles of human barbarism.

On September 19, the city had been abandoned by the Soviet forces retreating under the lightning advance of the German army. On the same day, Kommando 4a, an elite unit of the German *Einsatzgruppen*, the mobile death squads charged with exterminating Jews and other undesirables in captured territory, entered the city. On September 29 and 30, the squad, reinforced by Ukrainian police and volunteer Ukrainian nationalists who viewed the invading Germans as liberators from Soviet tyranny, completed the massacre of 33,771 Jews at Babyn Yar. By the end of the war, over 100,000 people, including Soviet partisans, Ukrainian nationalists (whose alliance with the Nazis was short-lived), residents of a nearby mental hospital, gypsies, Soviet sailors, and Dynamo Kyiv footballers, were also shot at the site. But of the estimated 100,000 dead, 90,000 were Jews.

The initial two-day operation was the largest single massacre of Jews during the Holocaust and took place a year before the Germans had initiated the practice of systematic mass killing of Jews by stationary gas chambers at three death camps in Poland—Belzec, Sobibor, and Treblinka.

The gas chambers were introduced in large part to overcome the psychological fallout suffered by German soldiers from carrying out mass killings of Jewish civilians at places like Babyn Yar. The killings in Kyiv were not achieved through train schedules, distant camps, and sealed death chambers attended to by Jewish prisoners. Kyiv was the stuff of crying children snatched from the arms of their mothers and having their skulls dashed against brick walls. It was the wounded climbing out from the piles of corpses and layers of soil pleading with their executioners to finish them off with another bullet lest they suffocate to death.

In the two decades between the massacre and the publication of Yevtushenko's poem, the official policy of the Soviet Union was to avoid mention of such massacres or else to deny their fundamental character as acts of genocide. Over 1.3 million Jews were killed in sites like Babyn Yar throughout the Soviet Union. Most remain neglected.

The Soviet authorities had good reason to deny the nature of these crimes. For one, an invading army freely hunting and massacring over a million civilians throughout the land made a mockery of supposed Soviet power. There was also the deeply uncomfortable reality that Ukrainians and other peoples cobbled together in the officially harmonious Soviet Union had in many cases been willful participants in the killings of their fellow citizens.

By the 1950s, the Soviet Union had also become the foremost proponent of anti-Zionism, provided the Arabs with arms, and stood in visceral opposition to the State of Israel. Soviet propaganda denounced the Jews as "rootless cosmopolitans" and "bourgeois nationalists" for seeking a homeland of their own in no small part because of the failure of European states to prevent their wholesale slaughter.

Under Stalin and then Khruschev, antisemitism had become state policy. Restrictions on Jewish admission to universities were applied, show-trials of Jewish artists were staged, and a regular debasement of Jews in the official press created a pervasive culture of vulgar "street antisemitism" from the schoolyard to the trolleybus. In this context, the Soviet authorities had no desire to elicit sympathy for the Jews by fostering an understanding of what had befallen them just a short time ago.

Yet, among the population of Kyiv, there was no doubt as to what had occurred at Babyn Yar or who the principle victims had been. A small, brave cultural elite in the Soviet Union dared to probe the matter further, determined to expose through the subtlety and majesty of art what no official record would admit.

The composer Dmitri Shostakovich was moved to set Yevtushenko's poem to music. Upon reading the poem, he remarked to a friend, "I cannot not write it." In his dictated memoirs, Shostakovich observed, "people knew about Babi Yar before the poem, but they were silent. But when they read the poem, the silence was broken."

The sum of Yevtushenko's words and Shostakovich's music was Symphony No. 13 (Babi Yar). It was first performed in Moscow on December 18, 1962 by the Moscow Philharmonic Orchestra.

But, in a state where laying flowers at a killing field was seen as criminal subversion, a symphony by the most celebrated composer of the day, the lyrics of which chart the history of antisemitism from show-trials to Anne Frank, could not proceed without incident. The conductor was interrupted during final rehearsals with a request from the minister of culture to drop the offending first movement. He refused. The singer was then conveniently called up to perform at the Bolshoi.

The TV broadcast was cut. Still, the production proceeded at immense personal risk to everyone associated with it, not least Shostakovich himself.

Today, the denial of the massacre of the Jews through enforced silence has been replaced by simply drowning out the genocide through a preponderance of monuments and counter-monuments to each group affected by Babyn Yar. This reflects the complexity of modern Ukraine and its discomfort with truly addressing how a community entirely assimilated into Soviet society could be plucked from its ordinary metropolitan existence and delivered to the hell of the ravine under the watch, and in part by the hand, of their Ukrainian neighbors.

But art has an honestly that is difficult to suppress. Through it, two non-Jewish Soviet cultural titans, Yevgeny Yevtushenko and Dmitri Shostakovich forced a reckoning with the past that no Soviet censor or lingering party official could suppress.

A Homecoming

Indifference in Kyiv Seventy-Five Years after the Babyn Yar Massacre of Jews[1]

There is something about long-haul travel conducted in solitude that infuses the mind with a strange kind of focus. As I returned to Kyiv for the first time, having left that place as a boy of three, and now a man of thirty-three, my mind returned again and again in abstract and discordant ways to family.

Over the years, whenever my thoughts have turned to Kyiv, I could visualize nothing more than a grey blur, like a ragged woollen jumper. The only image that retains any clarity in my mind is one that my mind has created. I can picture my family, the family with which I left Kyiv, forever preserved in our ages at the time of our departure, standing stoically in our winter clothes.

I also associate Kyiv with fear. Fear is the dominant sentiment that inhabits the stories of my parents and grandparents. The fear that my family felt when they were denounced as traitors and expelled from their professions for applying to leave the Soviet Union so that my brother and I could live in dignity

---

1   This article originally appeared in the *Australian* on October 11, 2016.

in the West. The fear they felt when grim, sneering bureaucrats flicked through their identity papers and their eyes settled on that notorious fifth paragraph, which revealed their nationalities to be Jewish. And the fear that my mother felt every day during her daily commute from work as the trolleybus crept towards that sacred, cursed place where in September 1941 the Jews of Kyiv were made to huddle naked on the edge of the ravine and wait for their turn to die. She would tell me how every single day, without fail, just as the conductor would call, "Next stop, Babyn Yar" (the name of that ravine), at least one passenger would cry out and cackle and lament, "If only they had shot all the Jews here!"

As Doctor Zhivago flitted on my screen and the plane's flight path showed us to be between the chaotic skies over Syria and eastern Ukraine, I thought about that ravine, just a block from where my family had lived, the place where I played as a child, and would soon be stepping once again over the thousands upon thousands interred.

Now, in Kyiv, the city was not at all like I had expected. In truth, I no longer recall what I expected, the real immediately displacing the imagined.

I suspiciously eyed the locals, scanning the faces in search of my family's tormentors and of those, motivated by larceny, hatred or indifference, who played their part in putting my people into the ravine. My eyes fell on an elegant young woman with ice-blonde hair in braids. Then a stout, grizzled fellow with a prominent brow, resembling an Olympic weightlifter; and an ageing bohemian with thick, flowing hair and an unruly goatee, who looked like Chekhov. All perfectly agreeable in their own ways. Finally, I fixed my gaze on a thick-necked vulgarian, cheeks sagging giving the impression of a permanent state of outrage, small, darting eyes, and a nose red from drink. I told myself that I had successfully profiled a Nazi collaborator but then I sighted his Gucci loafers, designer jeans, and Swiss watch, and doubt crept in. Maybe capitalism does civilize.

While in transit, I had resolved to run my fist through the jaw of anyone who called me a "Yid" but it seemed that the place I returned to was not the one I left behind. At any rate, the current trajectory of Ukrainian nationalism was more concerned with the Russian peril than the Jewish one. I stared incredulous at the Israeli flags adorning Kyiv's main boulevard in honour of the visit of the Israeli President and was bemused by the rolls of toilet paper with images of Putin on each sheet that took pride of place in souvenir stands throughout the city.

A cab driver laconically summed up the current attitude as being, "If there's no water in the taps, the Russians must have drunk it all," a new-age take on the old ditty that once blamed the "Yids" for all the ills of society.

Later, on the train back to the airport, I would overhear a local pontificating to his girlfriend about the arrogance with which "the Jews" conduct themselves. I recalled my mother's torment before delivering some words that caused the man to withdraw and that are unfit for publication in any language. That incident, poignantly my last interaction with a local, assured me that, sooner or later, the cab driver's new slogan would revert to its original form.

I rode the trolley-bus from the city center to Babyn Yar but alighted a few miles south of the ravine. There I was to commence my personal March of the Living, retracing the death march taken by Kyiv's Jews seventy-five years ago to the day.

On September 28, 1941 notices appeared throughout the city ordering the Jews to assemble at an entry point to Babyn Yar by 8 am the following morning with their "documents, money, valuables, warm clothes, underwear, and so forth" or face death.

Some chose to believe that deportation awaited them. Others simply obeyed. One witness described the wretched procession of "howling children, their old and sick, some of them weeping . . . with their bundles roughly tied together with string and worn-out cases made from plywood. . . ." Others recalled seeing pure terror on the faces of the Jews as they drifted to their deaths under the gaze of their Ukrainian neighbours who had lined the street to watch.

I thought about the testimony of a witness who recalled seeing a Jewish woman approaching the assembly point turning to a soldier and asking in German, "What's next?" "There is no next," he replied.

I walked alongside the wall of the old cemetery and remembered the account of Dina Pronicheva, who survived the massacre by jumping into the ravine a moment before the firing began and sheltering under piles of bodies before making her escape at nightfall. She described the moment she leapt into the abyss as like jumping into a "bath full of blood." She had observed German soldiers losing patience with Jewish mothers unable to control their screaming children, snatching the distraught babies away and tossing them over the wall of the cemetery "like a piece of wood."

I now stood where the victims were forced to deposit their possessions, strip naked in the autumn chill, before proceeding to the edge of the ravine in small groups. The victims were then made to pass through a tight cordon of soldiers with dogs where they were clubbed mercilessly before reaching the other side. Pronicheva recalled the soldiers "laughing happily as if they were watching a circus act."

Humiliated, wounded, bewildered, the victims teetered on the edge of the ravine, clutching their children and loved ones as they awaited the fire of machine guns and toppled into the void beneath them. Some were not lethally wounded and bled to death under a mass of bodies. Others slowly suffocated under the earth that was heaped onto the victims at the end of each day of killing. Residents heard the "ta-ta-ta, ta-ta . . ." of machine-gun fire from dawn until nightfall and reported that the killing site shifted and groaned for days after the massacre.

I descended into what remains of the ravine and gazed out at what is now a pretty urban green space with its once harsh peaks and deep gullies levelled out into gentle slopes by the 100,000 corpses that lie underfoot. Couples stroll hand-in-hand, youngsters guffaw and sip beers on one of the slopes, all totally oblivious to the scale and depth of horror that once occurred there, and has forever sanctified the ground upon which they unknowingly tread.

I left Kyiv a few days later, having seen the house where I lived the first years of my life and visiting the Soviet-era cemetery a few miles further north where my relatives lie.

But the object of my visit had been Babyn Yar. I had come there to, in some hopelessly futile way, honor those Jews, indistinguishable from myself in look, language, or thought, for whom the march to Babyn Yar was a final march of death and not a symbolic march of the living. I departed haunted by their memory and by the callous indifference to suffering all around me. I think only of the words of the Soviet poet Yevgeny Yevtushenko: "No fibre of my body will forget this."

Having Lived the Alternative, I Choose Democracy[1]

Last weekend I was given the distinct honor of addressing an Australian citizenship ceremony at which almost one hundred people, from lands as disparate as Cote d'Ivoire and the Czech Republic pledged allegiance to Australia and vowed to uphold the laws and values of our nation. They proudly sang *Advance Australia Fair*, many shaming the locals with their command of that elusive second verse. It was a moving occasion, and to play some small part in it was a privilege I will not soon forget.

The privilege was enhanced and made more poignant by the fact that twenty-five years ago, as a seven-year-old boy, I sat in the very building in which the ceremony I was to address was taking place, in one of the seats I now faced, and became an Australian citizen after having arrived as a refugee from the Soviet Union in the late 1980s.

It was an easy speech to deliver. I just told my story. I described how I felt as a child arriving in a strange and unfamiliar land, together with my brother, my parents, and my maternal grandparents. We were penniless and alone, utterly unfamiliar with our surroundings and with the ways of

---

1   This article originally appeared in the *Guardian* on November 3, 2015.

Australian society, and, initially, estranged from a population we were unable to converse with. We were filled with trepidation and anxiety. My parents knew that their carefully forged careers and degrees and diplomas attained with pride in the Soviet Union would count for squat in our new homeland.

My parents and grandparents quickly went to work scrubbing toilets and selling clothes out of car boots in far-flung markets. We relied a great deal on the charity and good will of other Soviet Jewish refugees who had arrived in Australia years earlier and were now sufficiently established to lend a hand to new arrivals and keen to offer measured words of advice or unwanted pieces of furniture, the latter generally more useful than the former.

I told the audience of the meager possessions we had arrived with, consisting mainly of clothing crammed into old suitcases and photo albums to remind us of long-dead relatives and the lives we had left behind.

I spoke of our former lives in the Soviet Union. Our Jewish ethnic origin had been stamped into our identity documents for petty bureaucrats to see and sneer at. We were denied the freedom to openly practice our faith, to enter certain professions or study at certain universities. Perhaps the cruellest injustice of all was that, for a long time, we were even denied the right to leave the Soviet Union and seek a new life where we would be treated with dignity and live free from persecution.

I wanted to tell the audience about the village in the Ukraine where my father grew up and taught maths and physics in the local high school. How his students formed a queue outside his office and solemnly entered one by one to offer condolences upon learning that their beloved mentor was a Jew.

"How could this be?" one of them said, "You're such a good person." Or how, as a boy, my father inquisitively asked one of the old matriarchs of the village, "Aunty, why do we call this open plain a ravine?" "Ah, my boy," she replied. "It *was* a great ravine, until we filled it with Jews."

But it was enough to tell the audience something of the freedoms that we lacked and our hopes for a better life in Australia.

Then I spoke about values and freedoms, the values and freedoms that I, with my migrant eyes, have discerned and can contrast with those of the place I left behind. I spoke of democracy, tolerance, and mutual respect as the accepted norms of Australian society. I spoke about the corresponding responsibilities I now assume as an Australian citizen, to protect these values and freedoms both for myself and for others.

I turned then to what I regard as values that are uniquely Australian; the "fair-go" ethos, which ensures that the extent of our success is determined principally on merit rather than by social rank or position or accident of birth. Then I touched on that complex, somewhat ethereal notion of mateship, which to me combines elements of mutual aid, camaraderie, and, most importantly, egalitarianism.

I concluded by wishing our newest Australians good luck, and extended my sincere hope that they discover the beauty of our land and its people and will feel the same pride and love for Australia that I do.

I have no interest in bellicose displays of patriotism or blind loyalty to the fatherland. I am suspicious of any secular or religious ideology that treats the life of the individual as expendable. This is the kind of thinking, taken to its logical conclusion, that fills ravines and marks identity papers.

Yet I am able to recognize my extraordinary good fortune in having become an Australian citizen and can take pride in the values—some universal, some unique—that have made our nation one of the most desirable places in the world to live.

As it turned out, I was not alone in making speeches about Australian values that weekend. Across town, leaders of the Islamist group Hizb ut-Tahrir (HuT) spoke on the same subject, but in a very different way. To HuT, Australia's national anthem and democratic values are tools of an oppressive campaign of "forced assimilation."

I find such views repugnant, primarily because I have seen, through personal experience, that they are utterly false. Assimilation requires migrants not only to embrace Australia's laws and values but also to discard completely their traditions and sense of identity with the countries of their birth. Australia makes no such demands. Learning the official language was essential to my participation in my new home, but forgetting my mother tongue of Russian was never expected of me or requested. In fact, possession of a second language is prized and I take pride in consciously speaking Russian to my infant daughter just as my parents did with me.

By becoming an Australian citizen I learned about our nation's extraordinarily rich Aboriginal heritage, and to be mindful and respectful of the ancient custodians of the land I now inhabit. I also learned about, and came to appreciate, the great gift of the political and legal institutions we inherited from Britain. In no way was I required to forget my own heritage. Nor was I expected to adopt the predominant religion practised in Australia, Christianity. My right to practise my Jewish faith and identify with the heritage of the Jewish people has never been questioned in Australia and I am afforded the freedom to study and practise my culture and faith to the extent that I wish. That is not assimilation but integration—the key to Australian multiculturalism.

It is our democracy, representative government, rule of law, and basic freedoms that protect us from arbitrary power, cults of personality, and supreme rule by secular autocrats or megalomaniacs who claim a divine mandate to rule over us. It takes a special kind of evil for any person to try to use our freedoms in order to destroy them.

While Hizb ut-Tahrir may lament that our democratic institutions and traditions safeguard us from those who seek to abrogate the freedoms of others and impose their tyranny on the rest of us, I choose Australian democracy having lived the alternative. I am also confident that all but an extreme fringe of Australian society, including our newest Australians at the citizenship ceremony I was honored to address, live proudly and assuredly with that choice as well.

Index

"With clarity and penetrating insight, Alex Ryvchin unravels the mystery of antisemitism, distilling the roots of this most tenacious and pernicious conspiracy theory into seven fundamental myths. By shifting emphasis from the 'why' of this puzzling and dangerous phenomenon to the 'how' of the mechanics of its transmission, Ryvchin points to the possibility of actually confronting and diffusing it. This highly intelligent and well-written work should be on the mandatory reading list of anyone seeking to understand the age-old phenomenon of antisemitism, but moreso, or for anyone concerned with the ethical fate of the human race."

— His Excellency Isaac Herzog,
President of the State of Israel

"A smart, concise, and very up-to-date guide to the world's oldest hatred."

— David Baddiel, author of *Jews Don't Count*

"Carefully researched and graphically expressed, Alex Ryvchin's *The 7 Deadly Myths* systematically demolishes those anti-Semitic tropes, deeply embedded in Western culture, that are once again surfacing with potentially deadly implications. A trenchant warning of the sort that was all too easily ignored in Germany in 1933."

— Victor Lieberman, Raoul Wallenberg Distinguished University Professor of History, University of Michigan

"Hostility to Jews and Judaism dates back over centuries. In succinct, well-informed, and lucidly composed chapters, Alex Ryvchin focuses on seven of the most persistent and deadly myths that fuel such animosity. Readers interested in a brief but illuminating explanation of many of the causative factors behind antisemitism will benefit from Mr. Ryvchin's vividly drawn presentation of age-old anti-Jewish stereotypes. For all of their irrationality, they hang on threateningly to this day."

— Alvin H. Rosenfeld, Professor of English and Jewish Studies and Irving M. Glazer Chair in Jewish Studies, Indiana University

"Alex Ryvchin has made a significant contribution to the field of antisemitism studies. In a very readable narrative, he uses seven of the most powerful stereotypes about Jews to encompass the history of Jew hatred and in doing so lends perspective to what's happening now. At this moment in history when antisemitism has found new life around the world, this is a timely and important work."

— Jonathan Greenblatt, ADL CEO and National Director

"Ryvchin is an invaluable resource in his knowledge of our challenges and what needs to be done to address them, as well as in his stalwart commitment to the future of Jewish community life. His book is clear, persuasive, and a pleasure to read. Ryvchin takes a complex and ancient hatred and shows us where it comes from, how it changes, and how it remains the same. Essential reading for educators, policy makers and anyone seeking to grapple with the dangerous rise in conspiracy theories and Jew hatred."

— Ronald S. Lauder, President, World Jewish Congress

Printed in the USA
CPSIA information can be obtained
at www.ICGtesting.com
JSHW011425091023
49904JS00014B/78

9 798887 193304